Rebooting
the Regions

Rebooting the Regions

Why low or zero growth needn't mean the end of prosperity

Edited by
Paul Spoonley

MASSEY UNIVERSITY PRESS

First published in 2016 by Massey University Press
Private Bag 102904, North Shore Mail Centre,
Auckland 0745, New Zealand
www.masseypress.ac.nz

Design by Jo Bailey. Layout by Sarah Elworthy
Diagrams redrawn by Janet Hunt

A catalogue record for this book is available from the National Library
of New Zealand

Printed and bound in New Zealand by Printlink

ISBN: 978-0-9941300-3-7
eISBN: 978-0-9941325-6-7

Contents

Foreword

New Zealand, like nations throughout the world, faces a period of significant change and uncertainty. These changes pose challenges for communities across the country. How we manage these challenges and the decisions we make today will have a direct bearing on our quality of life in years to come.

Changes to our climate, environment, demography and the nature of work will alter the ways we live considerably. Whether it's coping with increased urbanisation and what that means for both cities and regions, responding to climate change, or caring for our environment, big challenges lie ahead.

How these changes affect regional New Zealand will have a huge impact on the whole country. The theme of this book strikes a chord with the local government sector in New Zealand, where considerable work is under way to identify the major shifts and begin conversations with communities about how to build resilience and ensure everyone has the opportunity to prosper.

This year Local Government New Zealand (LGNZ) launched The 2050 Challenge, a discussion paper aimed at future-proofing our communities, which sets out what we see as the major challenges ahead. This piece of work has identified urbanisation as one of the major modifications we face. Having more people living in urban areas poses a big challenge for regional communities. Uneven economic growth has seen some regions growing faster than others, with some attracting population while others are losing it.

Auckland continues to develop into an international city, and Christchurch rebuilds itself from the devastating earthquake damage of 2010 and 2011. Auckland has been growing rapidly and is now home to 1.4 million people out of a total population of 4.5 million. The city needs to be able to meet the demands of its growing number of inhabitants. Meanwhile, the Canterbury region is undergoing a rebuild process and has been the focus of much central government attention and resources.

However, while Auckland and Christchurch are both critical to New Zealand's success, the country's economic growth strategy needs to consider the nation as a whole, and the needs of its regions. There is a possibility that increased regional connectivity, enabled by technology, and other shifts might reverse the trends the whole world is witnessing, but the best estimates show that, in coming years, a greater proportion of the country will live in cities.

Whether a town or a city is growing or contracting, challenges are present. The problems that Auckland and other growth regions face in terms of housing affordability, traffic congestion and the cost of living are well known. These areas need to expand services and infrastructure to support larger populations, and to do so in a way that is sustainable and does not overwhelm other community objectives.

Areas experiencing population contraction face a different set of issues. These communities need to make big decisions about whether, when and how much to invest in renewing large-scale, long-lived public infrastructure to meet the needs of an uncertain future population. In a rates system based on population funding, these investments are difficult.

Opportunities to reinvigorate these communities need to be identified and fostered. It could be through maximising the lifestyle options afforded by communication and transport technology. We need to find ways to develop our regional centres into environments that offer opportunities in education, employment and business, as places where skilled locals want to stay and set up business, and where skilled migrants want to settle.

These things are not easy to plan for, or to achieve. From LGNZ's perspective, a collaborative approach between local and central government and communities is needed to address issues of such magnitude. The challenges we face can be daunting, but decisions need to be made across the public and private sectors. Failing to act will not help us to create the prosperous communities we want.

How we make these decisions is critical and should include a 'whole of systems' approach that involves all decision-makers — local and central government, and the public and private sectors. This is not a new concept, but the scale of coordination needed is growing, and we need to share experience to develop better models. We need to involve communities in the decision-making process in real ways, so that the diversity of our communities is reflected in the choices made. And we need to be able to respond to the uncertainty that pervades all of these challenges so that we are able to incorporate an evolving evidence base and make 'no regrets' decisions.

The change that is occurring and the pace at which it is happening can be overwhelming. But what is good to see is that the discussion about how New Zealand adapts — and changes, too — is well and truly underway.

Lawrence Yule
President, Local Government New Zealand

Introduction

Paul Spoonley
Massey University

Introduction

The second decade of the twenty-first century is proving to be significant for several reasons. It began with the global financial crisis that confirmed a number of the characteristics of a society like that of New Zealand: the changing nature of employment and of the employment contract that reflects underlying shifts in production (where and how); the hypermobility of modern migration flows (including the reappearance of forced migration as epitomised in the Syrian crisis); the growing diversification of New Zealand (and the superdiversity of Auckland); the pressures and limitations felt by national governments attempting to manage globalisation and the impacts of what *The Economist* has called the 'third great divide' as computerisation and digitisation change how we live and work; and the stresses of a society in which the economic and social opportunities of its communities are on diverging paths. This book focuses on one aspect of how these changes are playing out: the implications for regions. Moreover, we want to emphasise the demographic drivers and impacts.

Given the extent of these changes and the way in which they are changing our lives, it is important that we have information that helps us understand the issues and options. We have combined with Massey University Press to provide some views and data that will hopefully help New Zealanders to understand these complex trends and dynamics — and to encourage debate about what we want to see happen. Not all of the challenges faced by regions are rehearsed in this book, but we do want to emphasise the challenges presented by the very significant demographic changes that will characterise this second decade of the twenty-first century. These trends have been obvious for a while — consider the structural ageing of New Zealand's population — but over the coming decade the number of those aged over 65 will double, the very high current rates of immigration will continue to drive population growth and diversity, and we will continue to see the implications of changing entry:exit ratios for the size and distribution of the workforce. Each of these demographic changes can be seen through a regional lens when it comes to implications for economic and social options. It is this lens that we use here to explore developments and the future for regions in New Zealand.

Sometimes, New Zealand is changed by governments. Sometimes, changes are imposed on us and governments tend to adopt a reactive mode. At the moment there are some significant changes that are altering the composition and well-being of communities. What are the options? Are there policy interventions that will achieve politically desirable outcomes? Is there a will, at a local or a national level, to moderate or change the negative outcomes that we are seeing? Is there agreement as to the nature and significance of these outcomes and whether they are actually negative or positive? This is our contribution to these debates.

1. Regional futures: Diverging demographies and economies

Paul Spoonley
Massey University

Regional futures: Diverging demographies and economies

As New Zealand emerged from the global financial crisis (GFC) after 2012, the country seemed economically buoyant, with jobs growth, a strong primary sector and population growth at 1.9 per cent. But although a degree of economic vitality and certainty seemed to be the order of the day or perhaps even the decade, anyone who bothered to take a closer look would soon have realised that this was not the story for all parts of New Zealand society.

New fissures and tensions were readily apparent. It is a particular dimension of twenty-first-century New Zealand that we want to focus on: the well-being and options faced by the regions. Through 2015 and 2016, as immigration rates peaked at a historical high, as dairying took a big hit in the prices received for milk products, and as the effects of wage stagnation, precarious work and insufficient pay reappeared, it was clear that a new New Zealand was emerging that encompassed quite different economic futures for different regions.

In one sense, this was simply the story of contemporary globalisation — whereby new centres of economic growth were located in global cities that were not necessarily the old global cities of industrial capitalism in North America and Europe, although some of these remained important. The periphery often became a story of decline as the Industrial Revolution was replaced by new forms of capitalist production and consumption — and the changes wrought by the Digital Revolution.

In this new order, some of the centres of Fordist production, like Detroit, were part of the rust belt with the resulting negative implications for economic and community viability.

There were also victims in rural and regional economies around the world, including New Zealand. Employment was increasingly in the service economy and growth was associated with knowledge work and the provision of services. Successful regions tended to be associated with the agglomeration effects of city economies that were a product of population and economic growth, co-location and new networks, and were internationally connected; those with gloomier futures tended to experience population stagnation or even decline, as well as relatively thin labour markets that struggled to obtain or retain skilled labour supply, and were often reliant on old industries and low-return activities.

These issues were highlighted in 2015 and 2016 by a series of media stories about such varied dimensions as the runaway and increasingly less affordable housing market in Auckland, the contribution of immigrants to economic vitality and the arrival of superdiversity, and the upsides of living in certain regions (which often appeared as a crude form of boosterism; see below).

As if to underline the new order of matters, there was also a series of reports on the impacts of computerisation and digitisation on the economy, production and employment. More on this soon. But the impacts on regions and what ought to be done became an increasingly important policy and political debate — and with good reason.

In the same way that individuals, households or communities were experiencing the impacts of these economic changes, regions faced a range of different futures, and were back as a key focus of economic development. Should the aim be to save them or to accept that there was an inevitability in the rise and fall of regions? And there was a new dimension to these debates: the very different demographic patterns and profiles that had emerged in the early decades of the century and which were to be confirmed over the next decade.

This book is an exploration of these dynamics and issues. It rehearses the demographic changes that will (re)define communities through the first half of this century. It examines the different economic drivers and outcomes that are affecting regions and the options available to communities. It highlights the relative invisibility of some communities in these debates, notably Māori. It explores the very different trajectories of our metropolitan areas, notably Auckland and Christchurch, compared with those regions that lack the growth nodes provided by large agglomeration economies, and it looks at some of the new thinking and options required, given the very different circumstances of the early twenty-first century.

In 1938, American economist Alvin Hansen coined the phrase 'secular stagnation' to focus attention on the possibility that declining population growth would reduce economic growth, especially as it would have impacts on savings and investments, limit the availability of workers and, as older people saved for retirement, depress consumption. Low aggregate demand would result. He could not have been more incorrect in terms of population growth, as the post-war period saw one of the most significant increases in the birth rate, resulting in the baby boom that was to define the mid and late twentieth century.

But in late 2013, economist Larry Summers reintroduced the topic and the result has been — at times — a highly technical debate among economists that has focused on a range of issues from low average increases in real wages and diverging incomes through to whether there are inherent weaknesses in the global economy given the reliance on financial bubbles (the latter being the argument that Summers is advancing; see Bossone, 2015; Summers, 2014 and 2016; Welde, 2015).

But the focus in this book is on what is happening in the context of a national economy and the implications for regions of population stagnation or decline (see McMillan, 2015). The combination of the GFC and the realisation that demography has become something of a game-changer has helped to focus attention on a range of policy debates and options, some of which have been around for a very long time. Krugman and Eggertsson (2014) link population stagnation to economic outcomes:

> . . . nature is [providing] . . . an incredible austerity policy, a non-fiscal contraction functionally equivalent to 7 per cent of GDP.

They point to the implications of population change and, specifically, an ageing population for a country like Japan or, more broadly, the implications as baby boomers age and the working age population shrinks. The reduction in population growth of one percentage point has, they argue, an equivalent impact on the GDP growth trend, primarily by reducing investment demand. They go on to argue that this depresses economies and that the depressed state of the world economy after the beginning of the GFC in 2008 is now the 'new norm'.

The shrinking of the working age population (historically defined as those aged between 15 and 64, although this too needs changing given the way in which entry into work has been delayed for many, as well as the fact that ongoing paid employment past 65 is increasing) means that there has been an impact on savings rates and investment, that output growth is tempered by the lack of workers, and that older people depress consumption as they save for retirement. These three outcomes directly echo Hansen's forecast of 1938.

It is interesting to translate the general premise of first Hansen and more recently Krugman and Eggertsson into the economic implications and trajectories for New Zealand's regions. As several chapters in this book make clear, regions face a range of demographically related challenges, the most profound of which concern those regions that are facing population stagnation or decline.

Those responsible for governing these localities need to consider a significant shift in approach from one of anticipating growth to one of 'no growth' or even decline — and what this means for policy and economic and community development, and what tools might make sense of the very different scenarios they are facing. As Bruce (2015) demonstrates, towns like Taumarunui, Tokoroa or Whanganui have all declined in the past two decades by 1000 to 3000 residents.

But the headline story of a transition from a twentieth-century story of population growth to flatlining or decline barely touches on the issues. Many of those areas that are experiencing 'no growth' futures are also facing very different demographic profiles.

First, they are increasingly dominated by older people (structural ageing). A town like Thames, for example, is an exemplar of what others will experience: rather than those aged 65 or over comprising 10–15 per cent of the local population, they might now comprise 25–30 per cent (or higher). The median age in towns such as Tauranga, Whangarei, Lower Hutt, New Plymouth, Hastings, Napier and Rotorua is all edging up, although in some cases this is compounded by the fact that the city is a retirement destination. The local population profile is now dominated by the presence of older residents.

Second, local birth rates might be modest or low so that the numbers of those aged under 15 might be at a historical low, and are certainly low in comparison with the older population. In many regions, those aged over 65 will outnumber those aged 0–14 years, a policy scenario that is extremely novel. Third, those leaving school are also likely to leave the locality in search of further education or work. Many of those regions experiencing 'no growth' also experience a bite out of their demographic profile, involving those in their late teens and twenties, that is often not rectified in older cohorts. They leave and do not return.

This is the non-fiscal austerity that Krugman and Eggertsson (2014) refer to. The demography for many New Zealand regions and communities in the twenty-first century is in sharp contrast to that experienced after 1945, when the baby boomers first started to arrive. As this bulge progressed through the education system and then into the workforce, there were significant implications for growth, both population and economic. In many respects, these impacts are now being reversed. And there are significant challenges in ensuring that local communities obtain appropriate services and that employers have suitably qualified workers.

Just to underline the extent of change (past and/or present), Natalie Jackson's figures show that some towns — Kawerau and Wairoa, for example — are already experiencing population decline, while about a third of territorial authorities (TAs) are currently in a 'no growth' situation, which within a decade or so will encompass about two-thirds of New Zealand's TAs. It is a considerable and imposing change. And it has a range of implications that are quite different to recent experience. It represents, in Krugman and Eggertsson's words, a form of population-derived austerity.

The new world of work

'The availability of skilled people in a regional labour market can be a major constraint on growth . . . Regional differences in the availability of skills are the result of a number of interrelated factors, including quality of available education, services, demographics, and both domestic and international migration' (Ministry of Business, Industry and Employment (MBIE), 2015b: 9).

Regional vitality and viability are closely aligned with the economic opportunities and employment available. One of the significant changes that has occurred since the late twentieth century has been the shift in how and where we work. As *The Economist* (2014) has noted, a revolution similar in impact to the Industrial Revolution is under way. The Fordism of a classical capitalism is being replaced by the impacts of globalisation and digitisation.

This was reinforced by a series of reports that emerged on both sides of the Tasman during 2015, including the Chartered Accountants Australia and New Zealand (CA ANZ) report titled *Disruptive technologies: Risks, opportunities — Can New Zealand make the most of them?*, the Foundation for Young Australians report *The new work order. Ensuring young Australians have skills and experience for jobs of the future, not the past*, the Committee for the Economic Development of Australia (CEDA) report *Australia's future workforce* and the New Zealand Institute of Economic Research (NZIER) Insight report *Robot nation? The impact of disruptive technologies*. All point to the impacts of digitisation and globalisation on local labour markets, and note that between 40 and 50 per cent of jobs that currently exist are unlikely to exist in a decade's time.

Globalisation results in new centres of production, typically in those countries and cities that have lower production and labour costs, while digitisation is altering who actually works or how they work.

It appears that mid-skill and mid-income jobs are currently the ones most affected as computers replace people, but low skill/income jobs will also experience impacts (e.g. the shift to self-checkouts at the supermarket) and some high skill/income jobs will also be increasingly affected. The CA ANZ report anticipates that a significant number of accountancy jobs will be disrupted by the ability to program certain tasks. And think of driverless cars and trucks.

In a labour market like that of New Zealand, there have been noticeable shifts in where people are employed. As the MBIE (2015b: 11) notes:

. . . there has been a shift in New Zealand's employment structure over the past decade, with a decline in manufacturing sector's share of employment, and an increase in employment in the services sector . . . This is an extension of longer-term trends and can be observed across most advanced economies.

As noted above, an increasing number of people are employed in service-sector jobs. By the 2013 Census, almost four out of five jobs were in this sector and health care had replaced manufacturing as the single most important sector in terms of the total number of people employed. The primary sector is still important, but has reduced in terms of the proportion of New Zealanders employed in it. And some groups remain disproportionately in those industries that are forecast to decline; Māori would be one such group (see MBIE, 2015d).

The efficiencies provided by new technologies and production systems have meant that more can be produced with the same or a smaller workforce. This has been compounded by the use of immigrant labour, either in the form of the Recognised Seasonal Employer scheme, which sees temporary labour from Tonga or Kiribati working in the horticultural sector, or the dairy industry's use of Filipino workers.

The move to service work and the decline in manufacturing or primary-sector employment has had an impact on many regional economies as low-income jobs (say in tourism) replace local manufacturing or primary-sector processing (the decline in the numbers of people employed in meat processing since the late 1980s would be a case in point). This is exacerbated by the relatively thin labour markets in the regions.

A useful test is to look at the number of employers who employ more than 100 people in any given region (this information can be found in the excellent MBIE annual regional report; see MBIE, 2105b). Typically, those who are major employers tend to be the local district health board, the local authority or perhaps a local university or polytechnic along with a smattering of private-sector employers. Employers often struggle to find appropriate skilled workers or the local economy might be very dependent on a small number of industries, so that a downturn in milk or oil prices, or the departure of one of those large employers, has a magnified impact on the local economy and labour market.

Population-based government funding tends not to be sensitive to particular local needs (with some important exceptions such as the loading for education or health when there is a significant local Māori population or deprivation, for example). Furthermore, those services that do require a certain population threshold — say a local school or medical practice — are often put at risk. The media story that appeared in February 2016 of a medical practice in Tokoroa which had failed to recruit a GP, even though an annual salary of $400,000 was being offered, underlines some of these challenges (*NZ Herald*, 24 February 2016). The regional situation contrasts sharply with Auckland where, as one example, the Ministry of Education is anticipating that it will need to find 107,000 additional places in the primary and secondary school system to accommodate growth over the next three decades.

The nature of the employment contract has also changed over the last three decades. The de-unionisation of the workforce, the shift to non-standard — and often precarious and low-paid — forms of work, and the individualisation of workplace contracts has meant that the twentieth-century expectations concerning work need to be adjusted. A traditional linear trajectory — education, training and then a career in a particular occupation or industry — has been replaced by much greater variety in the nature of the work experience and contract.

This is as true for city labour markets as for the smaller regional centres, but the effects are compounded by the mix of employment and the presence of those institutions — tertiary education, research and development, services — that drive the growth in new jobs and provide more core jobs (as opposed to those on the periphery in terms of pay or security). As the MBIE (2015b: 11) notes, the metropolitan economies have been the most advantaged because of the 'composition of their industrial bases', with large service sectors, whereas many regions with higher levels of lower-skilled occupations have seen at best modest growth and often a decline (see Johnson, 2015: MBIE, 2015b). This is further compounded by the drive towards labour flexibility (and hence a growing precariousness for many). The British economist Guy Standing (2011: 31–45) argues that this is reflected in the following:

— Numerical flexibility or the growth of non-standard labour, especially the use of temporary labour in order to downsize (or upsize) quickly.
— Functional flexibility or the ability of firms to 'shift workers between tasks, positions and workplaces' (Standing, 2011: 36.)
— Occupational dismantling or the ability of those in a particular occupation to self-regulate and maintain a monopoly (it is 'anti-competitive').
— Wage flexibility so that wages are 'lower, more variable and more unpredictable' (Standing, 2011: 44).

This tends to be translated into quite different regional situations when it comes to regions, as skills and industry mix combine to produce particular job growth and labour market participation rates. Johnson (2015: 43) suggests that there are four distinct patterns:

— Low growth and low participation (Northland, Bay of Plenty, Hawke's Bay–Gisborne and Manawatū-Whanganui)
— Low growth and low participation (Auckland and Otago)
— Low growth and modest participation (Taranaki, all South Island regions bar Otago)

— Low growth and high participation (Wellington region).

The past 10 years have shown that the regions of New Zealand are on quite different pathways in terms of jobs and incomes.

These different stories reflect the long-term trends associated with what *The Economist* (2014) refers to as the 'third great wave' or the third industrial revolution. *The Economist* asks whether more jobs will be destroyed than created. For the moment, this might be the case in some regions (the low-growth regions identified above) but is less true for high growth, notably in Auckland.

Auckland: agglomeration drivers and effects

If many regions are facing low population growth or no-growth futures, this is not true of a number of metropolitan centres — Canterbury as a result of the post-earthquake rebuild, Wellington (although growth will slow over the next two decades), Hamilton and Tauranga, and some other centres such as Queenstown — but the growth of Auckland is anticipated to dominate the population growth of the country over the next two decades. Sixty per cent of New Zealand's growth will occur in this city, which will have the effect of growing the proportion of the country's population resident there from its current 33 per cent to something approaching 40 per cent. (Between 2006 and 2013, 11 New Zealand cities were responsible for 75 per cent of the country's growth, with Auckland making up more than 50 per cent of this growth.)

As with other primary and internationally connected cities, Auckland is seeing the effects of agglomeration — the cumulative outcomes of population and economic growth so that scale and co-location prompt further and ongoing growth — of jobs, of services, of population and of economic development generally. As a result, Auckland accounts for 35 per cent of the New Zealand economy, is home to two-thirds of the country's top 200 companies, and has a 'critical mass of public and private research organisations (including world class tertiary institutions)' (MBIE, 2015b: 20); also job growth in the region for the decade 2004–14 has made up almost two-thirds of New Zealand's job growth (Johnson, 2015: 51).

Symptomatic of Auckland's growth has been the increasing concern about housing availability and affordability. In April and May 2016, the *NZ Herald* ran a series of articles that focused on the pressures and purchase costs of property in the city. As Fry and Glass (2016: 43) note, demand for housing in Auckland is a function of the city's popularity — and of the inability to produce enough houses at an appropriate price level — but the evidence is that net migration gains do have an effect on house prices. (The evidence differs; in one study a 1 per cent net gain was calculated to have increased house prices by 10 per cent, while another concluded that the house-price gain was 8 per cent; Fry & Glass, 2016: 43.)

By early 2016, the shortfall of houses in Auckland was estimated to be 40,000 and the annual required rate of building (about 13,000 houses per year) was not even closely matched by the actual build of 9000–10,000 houses per year. This has prompted policy debates, especially given that the Auckland housing market is growing at a much higher rate than anything else experienced in New Zealand. (O'Brien, 2015, notes that the price of houses in Auckland increased 70 per cent in the four years to 2015 compared with growth of 9.9 per cent in Wellington over the same period.) This meant that the median Auckland house price had increased from $250,000 in 2001, or five times the median household income, to $812,000 in 2016 — now nine times the median household income (see Demographia's 2016 annual international affordability survey). Shamubeel and Selena Eaqub talk of 'Generation Rent', and there is also discussion of a land or capital gains tax, stamp duty, limitations on negative gearing and restrictions on non-resident buyers (*NZ Herald*, 27 April 2016).

Liam Dann (*NZ Herald*, 26 April 2016) had an interesting perspective: '. . . how do we solve this? There is no shortage of potential solutions. What we lack is the political motivation to enact the right combination of these solutions with the kind of urgency that will have an impact. What's happening in Auckland is a slow-motion disaster.'

The debate about housing and its affordability and availability highlights the demands imposed on Auckland infrastructure by growth. It highlights not only the 'success' of an economy and a city that is benefiting from agglomeration but also the challenges of accommodating growth. It underlines the growing disparities within Auckland — access to capital and appropriate levels of income — and the disparities between Auckland and other centres as the city dominates the country's growth. As a story in *North & South* (April 2016) noted with regard to those moving to Hawke's Bay from Auckland, there are definite trade-offs. Housing might be more affordable in regional New Zealand, but there are risks in terms of obtaining employment or establishing a business; it was also noted that the five local councils in Hawke's Bay lacked a collective economic vision, especially in the wake of a failed attempt to amalgamate.

However, the agglomeration drivers having an impact on Auckland have some distinct upsides. Motu's David Maré (2016) points out that labour productivity is 33 per cent higher in Auckland compared with the rest of New Zealand, and there are benefits arising from the nature of industry composition and multi-factor productivity (high input levels), density (Maré refers to this as agglomeration elasticity), the availability of skills and the connectedness that arises from the diversity of ideas (what has elsewhere been referred to as an idealopolis) and people, including immigrants. An understanding of the different futures faced by New Zealand's regions inevitably includes a consideration of Auckland's population and economic growth, as it provides an obvious counterpoint.

Is immigration the answer?

The demography of OECD countries is undergoing a significant shift, and is typically characterised by the structural and numerical ageing of the population and lower fertility rates. This has been led by Japan and Germany, but many countries are now experiencing below-replacement fertility rates. New Zealand is not. It continues to experience a fertility rate that is about replacement level, but declining (see Natalie Jackson in Chapter 2). Accordingly, recent population growth rates for the country have been relatively impressive at 1.9 per cent per annum. But even in New Zealand a shift is occurring. The fertility rate is dropping and is anticipated to go sub-replacement at some time in the next decade.

Accordingly, the contribution to growth rates provided by the arrival of immigrants has become a more significant consideration. Immigrant arrivals to New Zealand and the net gain from immigrants was subdued during the global financial crises, but the arrival rate increased post-GFC, and by 2014–16, the number of Permanent and Long Term arrivals was the highest it has ever been in New Zealand's history. For the 12 months ending in April 2016, the net gain in population was 68,100.

These are headline figures and thus do need unpacking. For example, the net gain includes those on study visas who might not stay ('Permanent and Long Term' includes all those who will remain in New Zealand for 12 months or more — and there are issues with the veracity of the data; see Spoonley & Bedford, 2012), as well as New Zealanders returning to the country — and fewer departing. Nevertheless, these are very high inflows, and by 2015 they were the highest in terms of the size of the resident population. (The OECD average for the five years to 2013 was 0.6 per cent of the population; New Zealand's was 1.4 per cent, which is higher than the two other countries that are most similar in terms of immigration policies, Australia at 1.0 per cent and Canada at 0.8 per cent; Fry & Glass, 2016: 21.)

Immigration is increasingly a key component of population composition and growth. As Natalie Jackson is quick to point out, however, it does not compensate for the ageing of the population. She argues that even a trebling of current immigration rates would have little effect on the structural ageing of the population, although it would contribute to population growth. However, immigration has a series of implications for New Zealand and its regions.

Historically, natural increase (births over deaths) has been the major contributor to growth, including for Auckland (see Jackson, 2014). But this has changed recently, and certainly in the wake of the GFC. With very high rates of inward immigration, 40 per cent of Auckland's recent growth (2006–15; see Fry & Glass, 2016) has been the result of immigration as New Zealand citizens return or immigrants arrive, especially from key origin countries: India, China, the Philippines and the UK. The result is that by the 2013 Census, 40 per cent of Auckland's residents had been born in another country (the figure for New Zealand as a whole is 25.2 per cent) and if the children of these immigrants are included (i.e. at least one parent is an immigrant), then the figure increases to 56 per cent.

In addition, the ethnic composition of New Zealand has been dramatically altered in the wake of the 1986–87 changes to immigration policy. Again, by the 2013 Census, 23 per cent of Aucklanders identified as members of one of the many Asian communities that were to be found in the city. Even with conservative projections, the proportion of the city that will self-identify as Asian will grow to 27–28 per cent in a little over a decade.

This is in distinct contrast to other parts of New Zealand. Even though it has recruited a significant number of immigrants to help with the rebuild, Canterbury receives less than a quarter of the annual number of immigrants that Auckland attracts. A little over 10 per cent of Wellington's population identifies as Asian, less than half that of Auckland. Auckland has become a city that is super-diverse in terms of its composition, is increasingly transnational as people and businesses develop or maintain contacts with other parts of the world, especially Asia, and has significant ethnoburbs (residential concentrations of ethnic and immigrant minorities) and ethnic precincts (the co-location of businesses run by members of the same ethnic community). More and more job-seekers come from these minority ethnic and immigrant communities, and more of the Auckland economy involves businesses that are owned by members of these same communities.

Looking beyond Auckland, if regions are not attracting immigrants, then they are not likely to grow either in terms of population or in terms of business/employment growth, especially since the GFCs. (They might attract temporary visitors as either tourists or workers, however.) As ageing continues to change the composition of regions and towns, and as fertility rates decline, then immigration becomes an important source of people and economic activity. Regions that do not attract immigrants will struggle. In the case of Hawke's Bay, for example, there was a decrease of 1300 in the overseas-born population between 2006 and 2013. (This might be explained, in part, by the impacts of the GFC on immigration rates.)

One of the most obvious impacts of immigration is that on the human capital pool that is available to New Zealand businesses and the economy. New Zealand's immigrant recruitment and selection system is based on identifying the skill requirements of the labour market and then allocating points in recognition of those characteristics that reflect these requirements. About 60 per cent of approvals concern those who come under the skill and entrepreneurial visa categories. (Those arriving on a study visa have been an important part of this skill flow, and some will transition into permanent residents once they have completed their qualifications and have met the requirements in terms of employment.) The remainder are largely made up of those approved under family reunification, with a small humanitarian component, nearly all refugees.

These skilled immigrants arrive with a higher set of educational qualifications than the host population and provide an important source of skilled labour for a number of industries. This might range from the Filipino workers in dairying or elder care through to IT businesses which have become increasingly reliant on immigrants. There is also evidence that low-value sectors such as hospitality and retail also rely on an immigrant workforce. In addition to providing a workforce, these immigrants contribute to demand and consumption in various ways (think of the ethnic precinct that is Auckland's Dominion Road) that are sometimes rather interesting: one banal example might be the arrival in school lunch boxes of sushi in recent years.

Immigrants, especially those from Asia, are typically attracted by cosmopolitan centres, especially Auckland, which provide the employment that they seek and have co-ethnic communities providing a range of networks and services/goods that they expect. But immigrants are also changing regional New Zealand. The Recognised Seasonal Employer scheme puts workers from Tonga or Kiribati into Hawke's Bay to pick and process fruit, and Filipino workers have been a recent arrival to dairying which has had the spill-over effect of altering the numbers attending schools and churches (Roman Catholic) in places like Gore. Nevertheless, the benefits of immigration in terms of a skilled talent pool of workers or the associated demand/consumption that is generated are not spread evenly. Auckland is a major beneficiary, with Christchurch, Queenstown, Wellington and Hamilton being second-tier beneficiaries. This uneven distribution of immigrants is compounding the problems that some regions face in terms of population growth or stabilisation, or the availability of skilled workers or new businesses.

Does immigration matter in terms of regional options and opportunities? The answer is increasingly a 'yes'. Immigration contributes to population growth (although not necessarily at a rate sufficient to offset ageing), provides an expanded talent pool, contributes to economic activity and growth, provides a resource in terms of understanding overseas markets and the networks that underpin new opportunities in those markets, and contributes to the diversity and vitality of New Zealand communities. But the benefit of current immigration flows tends to accrue to some centres and industries only. And are there Treaty of Waitangi considerations in relation to current immigration policy or flows?

Despite changes to government policy (an increase in the points that can be earned by moving to a centre other than Auckland), New Zealand has yet to develop the incentives and policies that would distribute immigrants and the benefits they bring more evenly to New Zealand's regions.

Boosterism: the regions fight back

As the New Zealand economy emerged from the GFC, Auckland's super-charged growth became an issue, especially as the costs of that growth — funding new transport options, housing availability and affordability, the various costs associated with population growth that by 2015 meant that Auckland was growing by 60,000 to 70,000 people per year — became something of a national obsession; except that it was really only the obsession of those who had to manage it in some way or those who were part of that growth as Auckland residents. Otherwise, there was little sympathy and a degree of antagonism. Why should other regions care?

There are some obvious answers to this question, but one of the effects of the media's preoccupation with Auckland was that there were some counter-narratives that focused on regional growth, as if to say: why not live here, in my community or region? These ranged from the 2016 *Listener* article titled 'Boom town Tauranga's unstoppable rise' (Vaughan, 2016) to the *North & South* series of articles in August 2015 which took the 'temperature' of small towns. Some of the language was extravagant: 'Migrants flock to

Tararua' (*Wairarapa Times Age*, 30 March 2016; it transpired that there was a net gain of 60 people in 2015 after a net loss of 552 in the 2006–13 period). A number of themes emerged: the costs and conviviality of small-town New Zealand; the housing value that could be obtained in comparison with Auckland; the quality of life, with access to high-quality leisure facilities; and the need to continue to value and support regional New Zealand as opposed to the behemoth that was Auckland.

The commentary provided in many of these articles tended to reflect a degree of boosterism: our community and economy are doing very well, thank you, and in our own interests and that of New Zealand it is important that we continue to thrive. Even some of the non-Auckland metropolitan centres felt it important to re-affirm their role and contribution. As Chris Whelan (2016) of the Wellington Regional Development Agency (WRDA), noted in an op-ed: 'the success of Wellington's economy is important to the prosperity of New Zealand as a whole — and vice versa'. He went on to identify the challenges for regional economies: talent attraction, retention and growth; connectedness (local and global); innovation; and distinctiveness.

Wellington is an interesting example of contemporary regional politics. Auckland went through a process of local authority amalgamation in 2010, but a public debate and vote to consider something similar for the Wellington region was unsuccessful (as it was in Hawke's Bay). Regional advocacy and economic promotion are largely the responsibility of the WRDA, which Whelan heads. The tensions between fragmented political authorities and a collective body that seeks to ensure that the four elements that Whelan identifies above as critical to economic vitality and growth are met are always going to be a challenge. In effect, Wellington is not so much in competition with Auckland as it is with other regions and especially cities, both in New Zealand and, to some extent, in Australia. Of course, matters were not helped by the comments of Prime Minister John Key on

Wellington's growth — or lack of it. Population projections indicate that Wellington will still see modest population growth through to the 2030s, but this growth will slow noticeably.

When one reviews media commentary and local/regional economic plans, several elements that seem to characterise public understanding and debate become evident. One is the failure to engage with the changed circumstances of the twenty-first century and to accept that population growth is unlikely for many regions and localities, and that new approaches and paradigms are required to deal with population stagnation or decline. In this book, Rachael McMillan provides some interesting comments on the failure to understand or accept reality — or to adjust thinking and resources. There are options. A future involving 'no growth' is not confined to New Zealand, and there are some interesting approaches that provide positive options for communities and regional economies from some of those regions that are more advanced than New Zealand in terms of demographic transformation. There are examples of 'no growth' approaches to economic and community development in Europe and North America.

Another relatively common response is to emphasise that there are new people or new businesses coming to the region. Politicians and the media emphasise the arrivals, and yet trend data and statistics tend to tell a somewhat different story. Hawke's Bay in recent decades lost significant numbers of its teenagers and twenty-something residents, and while some returned in their thirties or forties, or sometimes at retirement, there was a long-term negative effect on the region's population profile, especially in terms of a locally available (and skilled) working age population. *North & South*'s review of regional New Zealand in 2015 noted that there was also a range of challenges: everything from the struggle to sustain a senior rugby team through to the lack of local services (GPs, police, education).

One story that did seem to have evidence supporting it was the spill-over from the Auckland housing market with Aucklanders buying property in other regions. Colourfully titled 'Exodus of the house hunters' (*NZ Herald*, 18 April 2016), there was evidence that Aucklanders were buying property in the cities nearest to Auckland: in the first quarter of 2016, 18.4 per cent of property sales in Tauranga went to Aucklanders, 17 per cent in Hamilton and 23.9 per cent in Whangarei. The evidence was accompanied by the following comment: 'The exodus of frustrated first home buyers along with cashed-up baby boomers and investors seeking better financial returns is being attributed to unprecedented house price inflation in our biggest city.'

The facts gave some support to the view that Auckland was becoming too big and too expensive — and that there was a move to relocate. But, in truth, Auckland dominates the growth statistics, whether they concern jobs growth or population growth.

Policy options

This report suggests that as a national community we need to plan and prepare for several historically significant challenges and to use such planning and preparation as the basis for a new regional development strategy or agenda (Johnson, 2015: 11).

One of the points made by Krugman and Eggertsson (2014) in relation to secular stagnation is the observation that much of what is occurring is new territory and requires new thinking and policy options. The current options are simply not appropriate. This is compounded, they argue, by a timidity trap — policies are not creative and aggressive enough — and complacency (no single event occurs which might force a change).

One of the New Zealand government's responses was to identify what might be done in one of the most affected areas, the East Coast. MBIE published the *East Coast Regional Economic Potential Study* in 2014 and then moved to identify growth opportunities in five selected regions — Tai Tokerau/Northland, Bay of Plenty, East Coast, Manawatū-Whanganui and the West Coast — to be managed by MBIE and the Ministry for Primary Industries (MBIE, 2015a). A useful summary of the government's Business Growth Agenda is provided by MBIE (2015b: 12–13), which contains a number of initiatives designed to encourage regional and Māori economic growth as part of a cross-government programme.

In the 2016 Budget, funding was put aside for regional research institutes ($40 million) and regional growth ($44 million). This remains a work in progress, but some of the most strongly affected regions are included; whether there is enough to prompt substantive change is another matter. As one commentator has noted, economic measures are going to have to work hard to offset demography (Buttonwood, 2014).

Internationally, the policy responses tend to suggest that to be effective there needs to be major funding and policy shifts and an attention to a range of dimensions, some of which are social as well as economic. A number of regions and national economies are looking to sustain growth in regions that are struggling, and there is no shortage of pro-growth narratives or policy suggestions. One commentator (Laurence, 2015) suggests that the key elements are:

— control over local economic strategy by local politicians, enterprises and communities;
— sustainability and the resilience of local communities;
— the distribution of wealth across the local population so that there are no concentrations in certain income groups or localities;
— and a clear route for individuals into the economy . . . so that local residents will be able to access jobs and business opportunities.

However, local control has particular dimensions in a New Zealand context. As Simmonds, Kukutai and Ryks point out in this book, mana Māori and mana whenua underpin regional partnerships — or need to — in order to provide a degree of rangatiratanga for local Māori. But, as they also note, this has seldom been appropriately written into the stories of regional development. The experiences of Andrew Judd, the mayor of New Plymouth, when he sought to get Māori representation on the city council were a salutary lesson about the reluctance of many to agree that such representation was important. These issues of representation and participation in decision-making are further complicated by the superdiversity of a city like Auckland. What is appropriate in terms of tangata whenua? And then what is appropriate for other ethnic and immigrant groups — alongside rather than in competition with tangata whenua?

The policy challenges have not been lost on regions, and many have established their own economic development agencies and plans (see an assessment for Palmerston North at www.pncc.govt.nz/plans-policies-and-public-documents/reports/economic-update-reports/). Whether these are adequate in the face of significant economic and demographic trans-formation, both local and international, and whether there is sufficient political leadership and vision, and collaboration with other regions or government, remains to be seen.

Conclusion

One outcome of the current struggle which some regions are having with aging populations, minimal population growth and high levels of dependency, is that their ability to support local infrastructure and services is diminishing (Johnson, 2015: 101).

Commentators like Shamubeel Eaqub (2014) have pointed to the significant and growing gap between those regions which are prosperous and growing and those that are not, and which, as a result, experience poverty and limited job and economic opportunities, and are challenged in terms of accessing appropriate services (see also Johnson, 2015). Part of this is a function of scale — a service-based and knowledge-focused economy is most obvious in larger metropolitan centres that are internationally connected — but as this chapter and this book emphasise, there are also important demographic drivers and considerations.

These regional stories and the divergence in options and opportunities are complicated by the generic shifts in production, ownership and employment globally. As *The Economist* has noted, the current transformational shift promoted by digitisation and knowledge work, combined with globalisation, is changing societies and economies. This transformation will displace some workers as computers substitute for labour, while many other jobs will be disrupted (CEDA, 2015). The options available to regional agencies, or even governments, to deal with such transformative shifts are often limited. This is compounded by population stagnation and the contraction of the working age population, especially skilled workers. There are options and strategies, but first of all an acknowledgement is needed of the extent and nature of current changes and what they mean for regions.

References

Bossone, B. (2015). Krugman, Summers and secular stagnation. Retrieved from http://www.economonitor.com/blog/2015/11/krugman-summers-and-secular-stagnation/

Bruce, G. (2015). Small towns: Have the good times gone? *North & South*, August, pp. 30–51.

Buttonwood (2014). Buttonwood's notebook. *The Economist*, 3 November. Retrieved from http://www.economist.com/blogs/buttonwood/2014/11/secular-stagnation

Chartered Accountants Australia and New Zealand (2015). *Disruptive technologies: Risks, opportunities — Can New Zealand make the most of them?* Retrieved from http://www.charteredaccountants.com.au/futureinc

Committee for Economic Development of Australia (CEDA) (2015). *Australia's future workforce*. Melbourne: CEDA.

Demographia (2016). *12th Annual Demographia International Housing Affordability Survey: 2016*. Retrieved from http://www.demographia.com/dhi.pdf

Eaqub, S. (2014). *Growing apart: Regional prosperity in New Zealand*. Wellington: Bridget Williams Books.

Eaqub, S. (2015). *Generation Rent*. Wellington: Bridget Williams Books.

Foundation for Young Australians (FYA) (2015). *The new work order. Ensuring young Australians have skills and experiences for the jobs of the future, not the past*. Sydney: FYA.

Fry, J., & Glass, H. (2016). *Going places. Migration, economics and the future of New Zealand*. Wellington: Bridget Williams Books.

Jackson, N. (2014). *Auckland — Key demographic trends*. NIDEA Briefs No. 1, University of Waikato.

Johnson, A. (2015). *Mixed fortunes. The geography of advantage and disadvantage in New Zealand*. Auckland: Salvation Army Social Policy and Parliamentary Unit.

Keown, J. (2016). Big sun, small mortgages. *North & South*, April, pp. 39–53.

Krugman, P., & Eggertsson, G. (2014). *Do we face secular stagnation?* London: IPPR.

Laurence, R. (2015). The pursuit of regional growth is not translating into local prosperity. *NewStart Magazine*, 5 October. Retrieved from http://cardiff.newstartmag.co.uk/your-blogs/the-pursuit-of-growth-is-not-creating-local-proserity/

Maré, D. (2016). *Auckland and productivity*. Presentation to Auckland Productivity Workshop, Auckland Policy Office, 4 March 2016.

McMillan, R. (2015). *Taking action on depopulation — strategies, intervention and peripheral communities*. Morrinsville: Natalie Jackson Demographics Ltd.

Ministry of Business, Industry and Employment (MBIE) (2014). *East Coast Regional Economic Potential Study*. Wellington: MBIE.

Ibid. (2015a). *Regional growth programme*. Retrieved from http://www.mbie.govt.nz/info-services/sectors-industries/regions-cities/regional-growth-programme

Ibid. (2015b). *Regional economic growth activity report*. Wellington: MBIE.

Ibid. (2015c). *Medium-long term employment outlook. Looking ahead to 2024*. Wellington: MBIE.

Ibid. (2015d). *Māori in the labour market*. Wellington: MBIE.

New Zealand Institute of Economic Research (2015). *Robot nation? The impact of disruptive technologies on Kiwis*. Wellington: NZIER.

O'Brien, E. (2015). London house prices have nothing on Auckland. Retrieved from http://www.bloomberg.com/news/articles/2015-11-22/london-house-prices-have-nothing-on-auckland

Spoonley, P., & Bedford, R. (2012). *Welcome to our world? Immigration and the reshaping of New Zealand*. Auckland: Dunmore Publishing.

Standing, G. (2011). *The precariat. The new dangerous class*. London: Bloomsbury.

Summers, L. (2014). Speech. Retrieved from http://www.economist.com/blogs/graphicdetail/2014/11/secular-stagnation-graphics

Summers, L. (2016). The age of secular stagnation. Retrieved from http://larrysummers.com/2016/02/17/the-age-of-secular-stagnation/

The Economist (2014). The third great wave. October.

Vaughan, R. (2016). Boomtown Tauranga's unstoppable rise. *Listener*, 5–11 March, pp. 14–21.

Welde, D. (2015). Why 'secular stagnation' matters. BBC, 2 April 2015. Retrieved from http://www.bbc.com/news/business-32163541

Whelan, C. (2016). Power of co-operation key to regions growth. *Dominion Post*, 23 February.

2. **Irresistible forces:** Facing up to demographic change

Natalie Jackson
Massey University

Irresistible forces: Facing up to demographic change

Introduction

By comparison with most of its structurally older OECD counterparts, New Zealand's population has grown at just above 1.0 per cent per annum over the past two decades. This is similar to the global growth rate, and well above that of Europe where the growth rate is now close to zero — the outcome of advanced structural ageing. However, New Zealand's population growth has never been evenly distributed over the country. Following the initial dominance of the South Island, by 1901 the majority of New Zealanders were living in the North Island; this has remained the case ever since. The south–north shift has also been accompanied by a growing concentration of the population in Auckland, accelerating in recent decades to amount to just on one-third of the total population at the 2013 Census.

Despite a popular perception that the main cause of this concentration has been migration, both New Zealand's and Auckland's growth has for the most part been the result of natural increase — the difference between births and deaths. For Auckland, natural increase has accounted for around 58 per cent of growth over the past two decades.

This is not to suggest that migration has not played a major role — indeed, where migration loss has occurred in rural areas it has greatly reduced potential population size. Rather, it is that the essentially invisible role of natural increase in driving population growth in New Zealand and its regions has not been given the attention it deserves.

The longer-term implications of this oversight will now slowly become clear, as population ageing — in many cases accelerated by the compounding net migration loss of young adults over the years — causes one territorial authority area after another to reach the end-point of natural growth. Thereafter, any growth will be entirely dependent on achieving net migration gains. In many cases this would require a reversal of a long-term trend, and in most cases it is improbable.

This chapter outlines the dynamics of population growth and decline in New Zealand in the context of what is known as the global demographic transition. It explains that the growth we have come to take for granted was never going to be infinite and argues that as population ageing unfolds, it will be essential to revisit and revise almost every rule, policy and practice related to population — which means just about everything.

Failing to understand these unfolding dynamics and seeking to hold back the tide will be counterproductive. As we transition from growth to decline, or at least to the ending of appreciable growth, growing areas and declining areas will compete for resources — unless serious consideration is given to dramatically changing the current approach of rewarding growth. It is not possible, at this stage, to say exactly what the implications will be in every setting. For example, having more elderly people than children is a very new phenomenon and we do not yet really know what questions to ask. However, two things are certain: population ageing will be played out at the local level, and there will be no 'net' effect. There will be different implications for providers and funders, and for different industries and businesses; a particular problem for regions facing population decline — or a declining ratepayer base — will be how to approach infrastructure renewal cycles.

Differential growth and demographic transition

Between 1996 and 2013, Auckland accounted for over half of New Zealand's population growth. Auckland and the three other fastest-growing cities

(Tauranga, Hamilton and Wellington) shared two-thirds of the growth, while Auckland and just 13 of the 67 territorial authority areas (TAs) accounted for over 90 per cent, leaving a bare 10 per cent to be shared among the remaining 53 TAs. Twenty-two of these TAs actually declined in size during this period.

Currently, the primary cause of New Zealand's rural depopulation is net migration loss at young adult ages; now considered to be the 'old' form of decline. Increasingly, and with some imminence, migration-driven depopulation will be accompanied by the onset of natural decline, the end result of structural ageing that is ushering in more elderly than children and more deaths than births. Together, the trends will become self-reinforcing as this 'new' form of depopulation takes hold. This is already the case for Japan and much of Europe.

This situation is emerging because the developed world is now coming to the end of its 300-year-long demographic transition, during which falling infant and child mortality rates initially caused populations to become more youthful and 'explode' in size, as births increasingly exceeded deaths and 'natural increase' soared, and then to grow structurally older, as more people lived longer and birth rates fell — ushering in the end of natural growth. Ironically, natural increase has long been taken for granted while immigration has been widely and incorrectly assumed to be the primary cause of growth.[1] The irony is that the forthcoming end of natural increase will see the ethnic (country of birth) composition of regions — and countries — change very rapidly as majority growth from natural increase *initially* gives way to majority growth from immigration, increasingly from developing countries.

———

1   For New Zealand, the decade 2004–14 saw natural increase account for over 321,000 people while net international immigration delivered just over 100,000.

Population waves, age structural transitions and ageing-driven growth

The underlying trends are clearly visible when population projections are mapped by age at TA level — although it is important to note that retrospective mapping (for example, across the period 1996–2013) reveals the same trends in their earlier stages. Projected change is shown below for seven broad age groups, for three successive periods: 2013–23, 2023–33 and 2033–43, based on Statistics New Zealand's 'medium-case' assumptions (which include a net international immigration gain of 12,000 people per year, across the country). Lighter-shaded and cross-hatched areas depict growth; darker-shaded areas depict decline. The inexorable movement of waves or 'age structural transitions' through the age structure is clearly discernible, with very few TAs proving resistant to the overall trend.

First, a caveat is needed. Between 2002 and 2008 there was a small increase in New Zealand's birth rate, which has since declined to its lowest-ever levels (1.92 births per woman). The increase in the 2002–08 period coincided with, and was in fact partly driven by, the arrival of a particularly large cohort of people at the main reproductive ages (25–44 years) — the children of the baby boomers. In 2008 the number of births was almost the same as at the peak of the baby boom in 1961; this spike can be largely understood as a second major 'echo' of the baby boom. (The first echo was when the children of the boomers were born; the second comprises the boomer grandchildren — although there was also a short echo around 1991 when the first boomer grandchildren were born.)

The recent 'echo cohort' is now (in 2016) aged 8–14 years. As these children pass out of this age group and into the next, the 0- to 14-year-old population will decline in a large proportion of TAs. In 2023, 45 TAs (67%) are projected to have fewer children aged 0–14 years than in 2013; in 2033, 55 (82%) are projected to have fewer than in 2023. Between 2033 and 2043 there is likely to be a slight easing of the trend, when just 51 TAs (76%) are projected to see decline in this age group. Overall, while the number of those aged 0–14 years in 2043 is projected to be 38,000 greater *nationally* than in 2013, 52 TAs (78%) are projected to have fewer. Auckland, a few Canterbury TAs and Queenstown-Lakes are the main exceptions to this trend.

The decline in the 0–14 year age group will be accompanied by a decline at labour market entry age (15–24 years). Currently, the population aged 15–24 years is declining at the national level as smaller cohorts born during the mid to late 1990s and early 2000s (following larger cohorts born in 1988–92) arrive at those ages. In 2023, 50 TAs (75%) are projected to have smaller 15- to 24-year-old populations than in 2013.

There will be a short respite to this situation between 2023 and 2033, as the recently born echo cohort arrives at labour market entry age. Their arrival will see a short-term and geographically patchy reduction in the number of TAs with declining 15- to 24-year-old populations (41 TAs [61%] are projected to decline). However, the decline is projected to resume between 2033 and 2043 and become geographically widespread as the trough that will follow the echo cohort in turn reaches labour market entry age (56 TAs [84%]) are projected to see decline at these ages. Overall, in 2043 there is projected to be around 24,000 more 15- to 24-year-olds *nationally* than in 2013, but 51 TAs (76%) are projected to have fewer people in this age group.

These waves or age structural transitions mean that the 15–24 years population will wax and wane at the same time as the number of those leaving the labour market increases, due to baby boomer retirement (or a reduction in hours worked). Together, these trends are generating a demographically tight labour market that will remain with us for several decades, despite anticipated reductions in labour demand in some industries and occupations; others, especially service-sector jobs associated with population ageing, are already seeing significantly increased demand. Regions and TAs with growth projected at these ages should thus not

Figure 1: **Projected percentage change in number of 0- to 14-year-olds:**

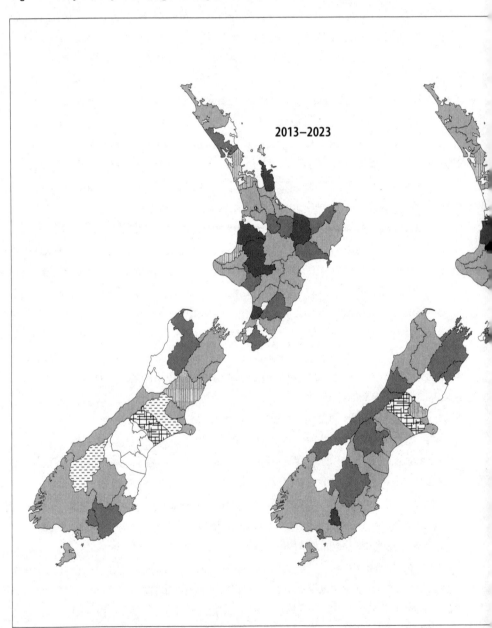

2013–23, 2023–33 and 2033–43

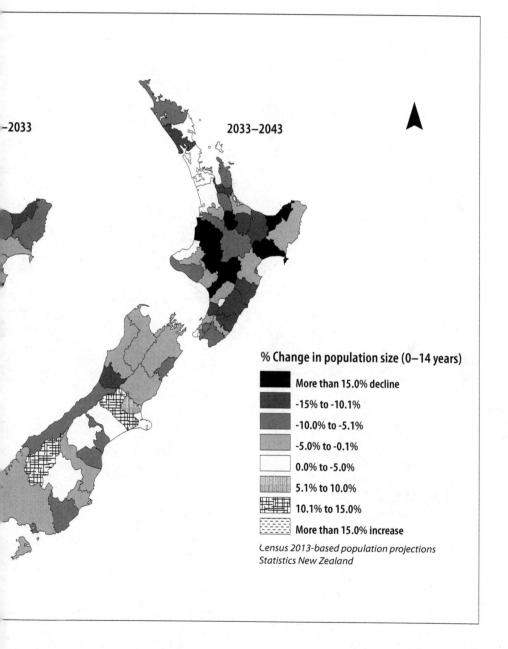

–2033

2033–2043

% Change in population size (0–14 years)

- More than 15.0% decline
- -15% to -10.1%
- -10.0% to -5.1%
- -5.0% to -0.1%
- 0.0% to -5.0%
- 5.1% to 10.0%
- 10.1% to 15.0%
- More than 15.0% increase

Census 2013-based population projections
Statistics New Zealand

Figure 2: **Projected percentage change in number of 15- to 24-year-olds:**

2013–2023

2013–23, 2023–33 and 2033–43

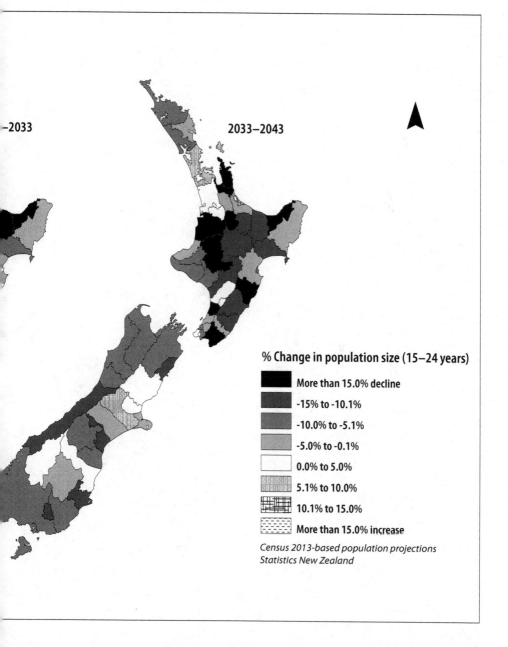

–2033

2033–2043

% Change in population size (15–24 years)

More than 15.0% decline

-15% to -10.1%

-10.0% to -5.1%

-5.0% to -0.1%

0.0% to 5.0%

5.1% to 10.0%

10.1% to 15.0%

More than 15.0% increase

Census 2013-based population projections
Statistics New Zealand

Figure 3: **Projected percentage change in number of 25- to 39-year-olds:**

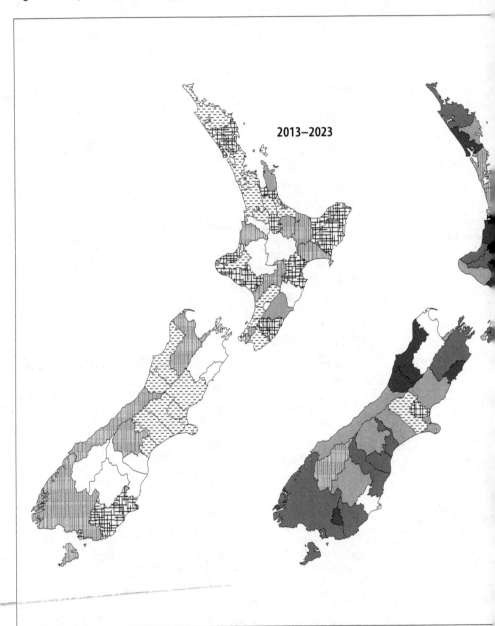

2013–23, 2023–33 and 2033–43

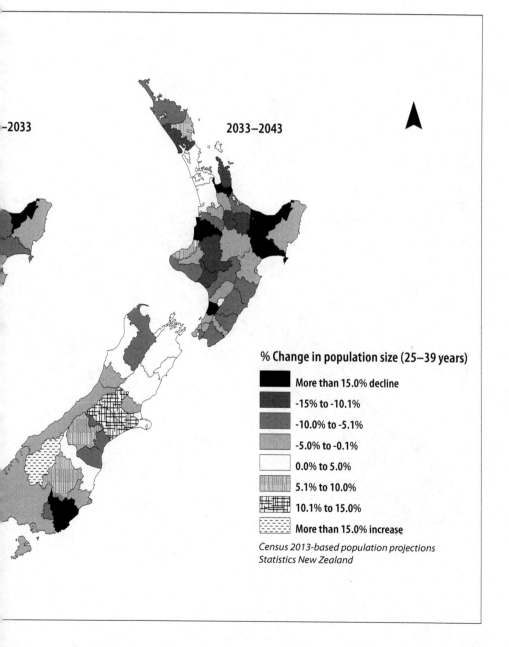

-2033

2033–2043

% Change in population size (25–39 years)

More than 15.0% decline

-15% to -10.1%

-10.0% to -5.1%

-5.0% to -0.1%

0.0% to 5.0%

5.1% to 10.0%

10.1% to 15.0%

More than 15.0% increase

Census 2013-based population projections
Statistics New Zealand

Figure 4: **Projected percentage change in number of 40- to 54-year-olds:**

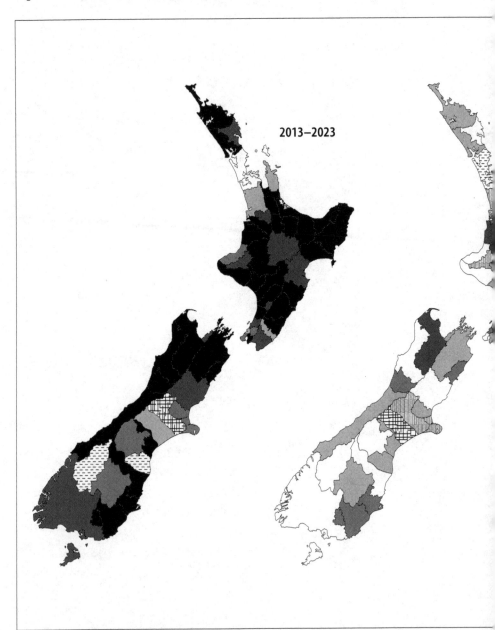

2013–23, 2023–33 and 2033–43

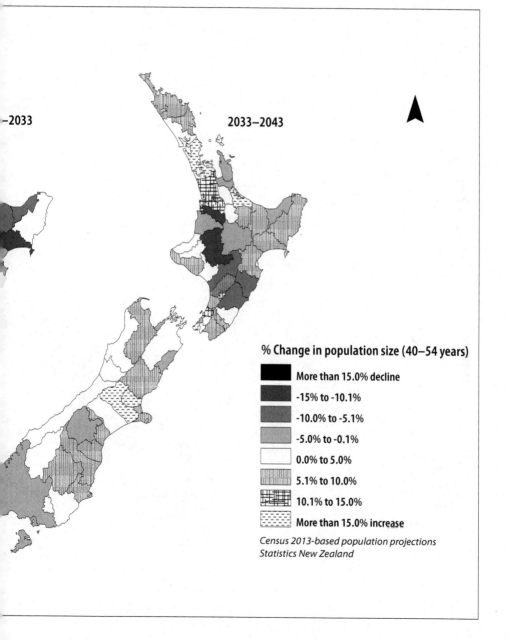

–2033

2033–2043

% Change in population size (40–54 years)

- More than 15.0% decline
- -15% to -10.1%
- -10.0% to -5.1%
- -5.0% to -0.1%
- 0.0% to 5.0%
- 5.1% to 10.0%
- 10.1% to 15.0%
- More than 15.0% increase

Census 2013-based population projections
Statistics New Zealand

Figure 5: **Projected percentage change in number of 55- to 64-year-olds:**

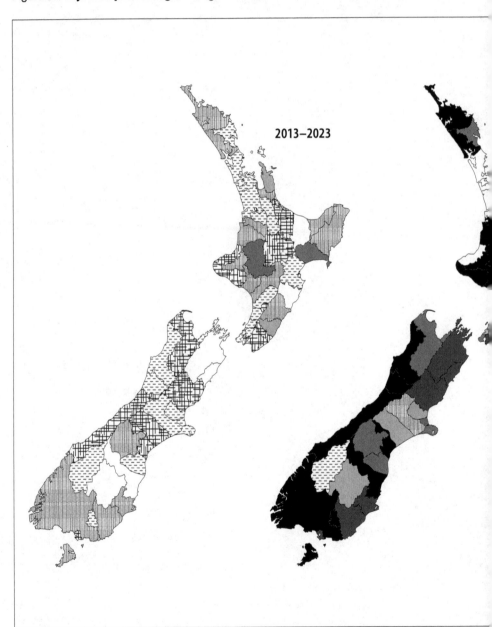

2013–2023

2013–23, 2023–33 and 2033–43

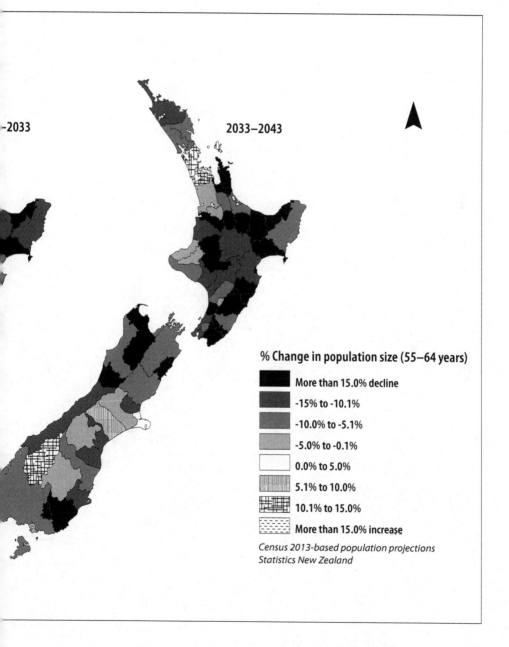

–2033

2033–2043

% Change in population size (55–64 years)

More than 15.0% decline

-15% to -10.1%

-10.0% to -5.1%

-5.0% to -0.1%

0.0% to 5.0%

5.1% to 10.0%

10.1% to 15.0%

More than 15.0% increase

*Census 2013-based population projections
Statistics New Zealand*

Figure 6: **Projected percentage change in number of 65- to 74-year-olds:**

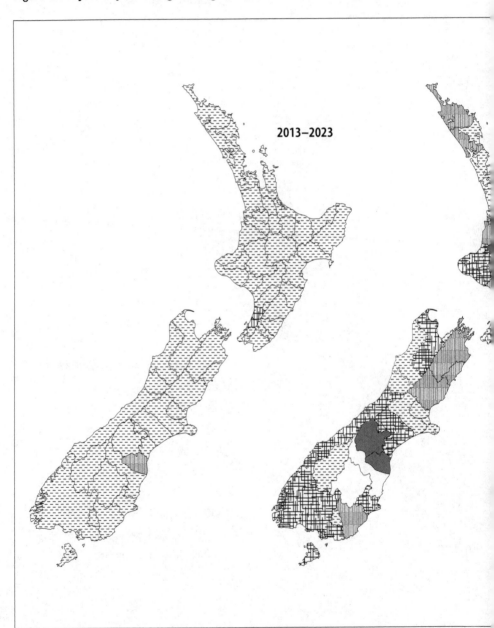

2013–23, 2023–33 and 2033–43

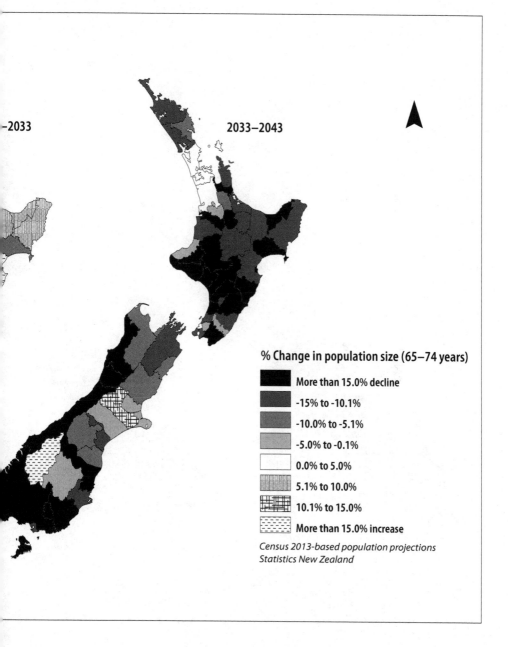

–2033

2033–2043

% Change in population size (65–74 years)

More than 15.0% decline

-15% to -10.1%

-10.0% to -5.1%

-5.0% to -0.1%

0.0% to 5.0%

5.1% to 10.0%

10.1% to 15.0%

More than 15.0% increase

Census 2013-based population projections
Statistics New Zealand

Figure 7: **Projected percentage change in number of 75+-year-olds:**

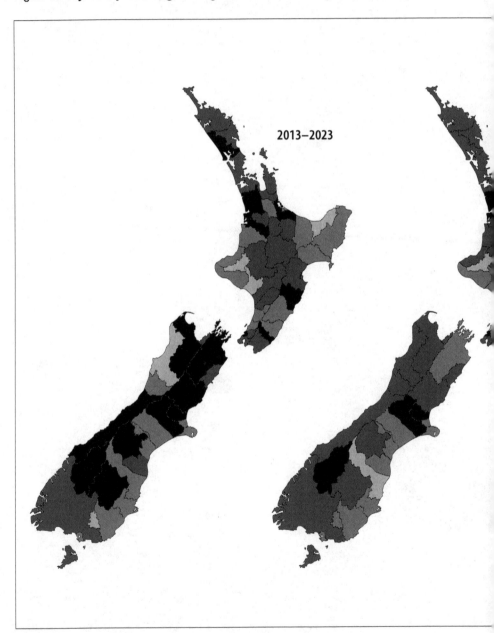

2013–2023

2013–23, 2023–33 and 2033–43

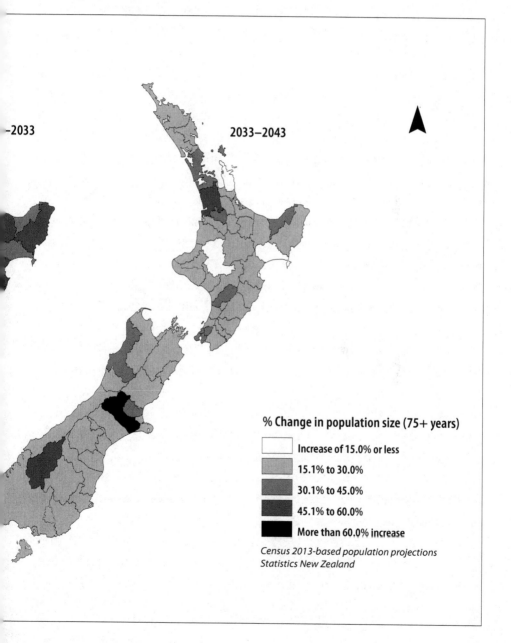

–2033

2033–2043

% Change in population size (75+ years)

Increase of 15.0% or less

15.1% to 30.0%

30.1% to 45.0%

45.1% to 60.0%

More than 60.0% increase

Census 2013-based population projections
Statistics New Zealand

become complacent — competition for internal labour supply will almost certainly increase, and the decline spans broad labour market areas (which include people commuting across TA boundaries) as well as TAs.

In contrast to the younger age groups, the 25–39 year population is initially projected to grow in most TAs over the next decade, primarily because the large cohort born around 1988–92 and currently in its mid to late twenties (the first of the boomers' grandchildren) will be passing through these ages but also, in part, because these age groups are those most positively affected by international immigration.

Between 2013 and 2023 only three TAs (4.5%) are projected to see a decline in the 25–39 years age group (these are Thames-Coromandel, Tararua and the Chatham Islands). Between 2023 and 2033 that number is projected to escalate to 50 TAs (75%), while between 2033 and 2043 it will reduce slightly to around 46 TAs (69%). Overall, 2043 is likely to see around 30 TAs (45%) with fewer people aged 25–39 years than in 2013, while the number at these ages is projected to grow nationally by around 212,000.

In complete contrast to the changes projected for the next decade at 25–39 years of age, very few TAs can expect to see growth at 40–54 years. Nationally, numbers will decline by around 61,000. This is because the largest baby boomer cohorts, currently aged 50–54 years, are in the process of vacating this demographic and moving into the 55–59 year age group. They are also followed by somewhat smaller post-boom cohorts, so the initial decline will be pronounced. Between 2013 and 2023, 64 TAs (93%) can expect to see decline in this broad age group. Between 2023 and 2033 the decline will lessen to around 41 TAs (61%) — and be accompanied by growth of around 82,000 people aged 40–54 years nationally — while between 2033 and 2043 decline at these ages is expected to affect just 18 TAs (27%). By then, the relatively large cohorts born in the years 1988–92 will be at those ages and, along with assumed international migration gains over the period, will result in around 138,000 more people aged 40–54 years nationally than in

2013. However, 55 TAs (82%) will have fewer people in this age group.

The pattern of growth and decline as cohorts move on to each successively older age group will now be clear. Because the baby boom (officially recognised as occurring between 1946 and 1965)[2] spanned at least two decades, trends at 55–64 years are almost a mirror image of those at 40–54 years. Initially there will be significant growth as the largest (youngest) boomer cohorts move into the 55–64 year age group, but this will be followed by decline as they then move on to older ages. Between 2013 and 2023 all but four TAs will see growth at 55–64 years (Thames-Coromandel, Ruapehu, Masterton and Wairoa). However, between 2023 and 2033, 60 TAs (90%) will see a decline at these ages, increasing slightly to 62 TAs (93%) between 2033 and 2043. Nationally, in 2043 there is projected to be around 69,000 more people aged 55–64 years than in 2013, but 52 TAs (78%) are projected to have fewer people in this age group.

The impact of population ageing and its accompanying age structural transitions becomes very clear with those aged 65 years and more. The immediate period (2013–23) will see massive growth at 65–74 years as the oldest/leading-edge baby boomers move into and through this broad age group. Between 2013 and 2023 all TAs will experience sizeable growth in this demographic; in only two is that growth likely to be less than 10 per cent (Kawarau and Waimate). The period 2023–33 will see further growth at these ages in all but four TAs (Thames-Coromandel, Ruapehu, Masterton and Wairoa), while the period 2033–43 will see an abrupt shift to the onset of decline at these ages in 60 TAs (90%) as the leading-edge boomers move on to the oldest ages. However, importantly (although not shown by these maps), by the end of the projection period all but six TAs (Kawerau, Opotiki,

2   New Zealand's baby boom actually began a few years earlier and continued for longer than this, but to save a lengthy explanation we are working here with the 'official' (USA) periodicity.

Ruapehu, Waitomo, Rangitikei and Wairoa) will still have more people aged 65–74 years than in 2013. Although the numbers will be diminishing, they will still be high relative to 2013 (+202,000) because of the sustained but slowing growth across the earlier period (2023–33).

The picture of sustained — albeit slowing — growth in the older population is very clear at 75+ years. No TA is projected to experience a reduction in numbers at 75+ years across any of the three periods. Between 2033 and 2043 there is somewhat reduced growth in a minority of TAs, but in 2043 there are only two TAs where numbers are not projected to have at least doubled over their 2013 base: Kawerau and Stratford. Nationally, numbers at 75+ years are projected to have trebled.

From these data, the Tai Timu Tangata research team[3] has begun to develop a typology of growth and decline. Using projected 'components of change' (natural increase and net immigration, based on the medium-case projection assumptions), we find three types of growing area and three types of declining area.

1. Between 2013 and 2018, 39 TAs are projected to experience growth from both natural increase and net immigration. By 2038–43 this situation is projected to relate to just 12 TAs.

2. Growth where natural increase is projected to more than offset underlying zero or net migration loss will apply to around 14 TAs in 2013–18. By 2038–43 this situation is projected to be the case for just three TAs.

3. Growth where net migration gain is projected to more than offset

---

3   Investigating a Royal Society Marsden project: 'The subnational mechanisms of the ending of population growth. Towards a theory of depopulation'. The Māori title is 'Tai timu tangata. Taihoa e?' which translates approximately as 'The ebbing of the human tide – what will it mean for the people?'.

zero natural increase or natural decline will apply to just three TAs in 2013–18, as this situation (of natural decline) is only just emerging. By 2038–43, migration gain offsetting underlying natural decline will pertain to around eight TAs.

4. Declining areas, where net migration will be positive but insufficient to offset natural decline, is not observed in the period 2013–18, again because so few areas yet experience natural decline. By 2038–43 this situation (net migration gain failing to offset natural decline) will relate to around 15 TAs.

5. Decline where natural increase is positive but insufficient to offset net migration loss is projected to occur for around 11 TAs in 2013–18. By 2038–43 it will apply to around 14 TAs.

6. Decline from both net migration loss and natural decline is not observed in the 2013–18 period but will be the case for around 15 TAs by 2038–43.

In summary, the number of TAs projected to experience depopulation will increase from 12 (18%) between 2013 and 2023 to 39 (58%) between 2033 and 2043, with another four (6%) at zero growth between 2033 and 2043, up from two (3%) in the 2013–23 period. By the end of the period, the depopulating TAs will account for almost 22 per cent of New Zealand's projected population of 5.64 million, up from just 5 per cent across the 2013–23 period.[4] This situation has implications for — among many other

---

4   It should also be noted that the projection of 12 TAs (18%) declining across the 2013–18 period represents a halving of the number observed to decline between 1996 and 2013, and is driven by Statistics New Zealand's very high net migration assumptions for the 2013–18 period. Currently, net international migration is around those projected levels and thus it is likely that such gains will be realised, at least nationally. At subnational level, however, they are also affected by the internal migration assumptions, and the international movements give no insight into the current strength or otherwise of those internal flows.

things — New Zealand's historical approach to funding local infrastructure from rates revenue.

Labour market implications

The trends outlined above have implications beyond just future population growth or decline. Bringing them together for the prime working age group (15–64 years), we can anticipate widespread shrinkage for many TAs while, nationally, overall numbers are projected to grow. Between 2013 and 2023 the prime working age populations of around 41 TAs (61%) are projected to decline in size while overall numbers grow nationally by 8 per cent. Between 2023 and 2033 this decline extends to 55 TAs (82%), and between 2033 and 2043 to 59 TAs (88%), while overall growth in numbers continues at the national level. By 2043 the working age populations of 51 TAs (76%) are projected to be smaller than in 2013, while overall numbers at these ages are projected to be 15.3 per cent greater. By 2043, growth at these ages will be experienced by just 16 TAs (24%), the vast majority of it (94%) occurring in just 5 TAs: Auckland, Hamilton City, Christchurch City, Tauranga City and Selwyn District.

Importantly, increasing the prime working age population by extending the upper bound to 69 years (and, appropriately, the main entry age to 20 years) does little to alter these trends. Between 2013 and 2023, the 20–69 year working age populations of 28 TAs (42%) would decline, increasing to 52 TAs (78%) between 2023 and 2033, and to 55 TAs (82%) in the period 2033–43. In 2043 the working age populations of 50 TAs (75%) would be smaller than in 2013, compared with 51 TAs (76%) under the 15–64 years working age parameter.

Workforce ageing is also accelerating, with many industries and most professional occupations already having substantially fewer people employed at entry age (here 15–29 years) than those in the 'retirement zone' (55+ years); this is known as the 'entry:exit ratio'. In 2013, 23.6 per cent of the employed labour force was aged 55+ years and there were just 9 people aged 15–29 years for every 10 at 55+ years of age. In 1996, only 11.5 per cent were aged 55+ years and there were 27 people at labour market entry age (15–29 years) for every 10 in the retirement zone (55+ years).

It is not possible in this chapter to go into the seriously low entry:exit ratios already observed in a large proportion of New Zealand's industries and occupations, but the four largest industries at three-digit level (at which 158 industries are enumerated[5]) in 2013 give an indication (again using employee age ratios based on 15–29:55+ years):

1. School education 4:10
2. Government administration 6:10
3. Hospitals and nursing homes 5:10
4. Marketing and business management services 9:10.

As a general guide, all of the industries concerned with health, community care, teaching, grain/sheep/beef farming, horticulture and transport have entry:exit ratios of around 3–5:10. In contrast, industries such as retail, hospitality and computer services have relatively young age structures — but it goes without saying that people are not perfect substitutes for each other and most lateral movements (e.g. between occupations, between industries) involve related training. As structural ageing progresses, we can anticipate growing skill shortages and competition for labour as well as decreased unemployment (both are already evident in the older regions, across New Zealand and several counterpart countries) and this situation

5   Customised Census Database sourced from Statistics New Zealand; includes Area of Usual Residence, Industry (ANZSIC96 V4.1) and Status in Employment by Age Group and Sex for the Employed Census Usually Resident Population Count Aged 15+ Years, 1996, 2001, 2006 and 2013.

can be expected to increase labour costs.

It should also be noted that older regions in general tend to have slightly lower labour market entry : exit ratios across most industries and occupations, and younger regions slightly higher. As indicated earlier, it is certainly the case that ongoing technological and industrial change will see the demise of many jobs; but it is equally certain that there will be increased demand in some industries, while capacity to physically — and fiscally — supply will diminish.

For example, New Zealand's community care services workforce has doubled in size since 1996, rising from seventeenth largest (at three-digit level) to sixth largest in 2013; other health services have risen from twenty-seventh to ninth; computer services from fifty-third to fifteenth; technical services from twenty-ninth to twentieth; and medical and dental services from thirty-seventh to twenty-seventh. Over the past 17 years, growth in such ascending industries has more than offset the decline in sunset industries, with a net increase of 370,000 jobs.

Can we hold back the ebbing of the human tide?

The inexorable trends described above are unlikely to be resolved by either international immigration or an increase in the birth rate. The number of migrants required to offset structural ageing is simply too large, while competition for them is growing — across the 58 more developed countries (from which most skilled migrants are currently obtained), the population aged 0–64 years is projected to be around 41 million smaller in 2031 than in 2011. In short, many of New Zealand's previous source countries, the now ageing and depopulating regions of Europe, are already competing with us for migrants. It should also be remembered that migrants grow old, too — over 30 per cent of today's older New Zealanders were once migrants.

In terms of fertility, it is currently a challenge to achieve an average of even two births per woman. With New Zealand's median age at childbirth now above 30 years, and one-third of the population already aged over 50, the nation's reproductive potential is rapidly reducing (albeit not yet as greatly as in our OECD counterpart countries). It is also worth noting that over half of all births at the peak of New Zealand's baby boom were to women aged less than 25 years; this distinction now falls to their older counterparts. Most obviously, however — as the maps above illustrate — a rise in the birth rate takes 20 years to generate additional workers. In the interim, New Zealand would be faced with a simultaneous increase in notional dependency at both ends of the age structure.

Projected labour supply shortages are also unlikely to be resolved in New Zealand by further major increases in labour force participation at older ages; of the OECD countries, New Zealand already has the second-highest employment rates at 50–64 years and the fourth-highest at 65–69 years, and these have already trebled since 1996. Outside of Auckland, there is minimal elasticity. Most of New Zealand now faces a demographically tight labour market that will persist until at least the mid 2020s, when the recently born echo cohort will be at workforce entry age. Irrespective of likely increases in the length of the working life, there is an urgent need for a national workforce planning strategy, along with decentralisation and other related policy initiatives to slow — or at least manage — rural and regional decline.

Since New Zealand has a relatively young age structure by comparison with most of its OECD counterparts, we might then look to them to see how similar issues are being approached. Recurring points from the literature — as outlined by Rachael McMillan in Chapter 9 — are that regions where population decline is most pronounced are those that are based on the 'old' economy; that towns are like businesses and need to reinvent themselves as their original (e.g. industrial) functions change; and that the market is not able to resolve either the demographic forces associated with changing industrial demand or the demographic forces of population ageing *per se*. As McMillan shows, policy interventions seem to hold most promise when they move from single-sector approaches (like focusing on employment and/or large industries or employers) to cross-institutional, cooperative, multi-sector approaches that focus on the locality — and particularly involve making 'place' as attractive as possible. If people are in short supply, they will go to (or be attracted to stay in) places that afford them the lifestyle they desire.

The overall message is that major demographic shifts are coming to a region near you. There is little that can be done to alter the demographic future, but much that can be done to ensure that policies are fit for purpose.

It is essential that regions and organisations or business sectors revisit their policies and plans, and the principles on which they are based, to ensure that they are appropriate for an ageing population — and to ensure that they consider the impacts and possibilities of the markedly younger and older populations within the overall population, such as Māori and European, each with different needs and opportunities.

How to engage with these trends and circumstances will very much determine whether regions, TAs and organisations will be successful. The quality of life and the attractiveness of place will increasingly become key determinants for sustaining population.

This does not imply a return to past levels of population growth, but rather, the maintenance of a stable population. Japan and Germany, for example, are two depopulating countries now implementing 'accepting strategies' that acknowledge the inevitability of population decline and seek to ensure the sustainability of smaller local populations, rather than trying to reverse the tide.

Knowing what the local drivers of demographic change are, and what can and can't be achieved in terms of population growth, is a first vital step for all councils, organisations and business sectors to engage with.

3. Here to stay: Reshaping the regions through mana Māori

Naomi Simmonds (Raukawa, Ngāti Huri), Tahu Kukutai (Waikato, Ngāti Maniapoto and Te Aupōuri) and John Ryks
Te Whare Wananga o Waikato / The University of Waikato

Here to stay: Reshaping the regions through mana Māori

Situated 65 kilometres south-east of Hamilton, Putāruru (population 3747 in the 2013 Census) is typical of the many farming service towns scattered across rural Aotearoa New Zealand. Bakeries, op shops, a sports bar and a farm equipment supplier occupy the main street. Unlike nearby Tirau, which transformed from a one-stop shop into a vibrant boutique village in the late 1990s, Putāruru township remains largely indistinguishable from other rural centres. There are few clues to the substantial farming-based and water-generated wealth that lies beyond the town.

Many locals have it that Putāruru is the 'home of the owl', on account of its original Māori name Puta-a-ruru. Puta means 'to come forth' and the ruru or morepork is a native owl. In fact, the town's name has nothing to do with owls; it originates from a story that establishes the territorial rights of Raukawa iwi over the South Waikato region. After the murder of Raukawa's granddaughter Korekore (sometimes referred to as Koroukore) by Ngāti Kahupungapunga, her attendant Ruru fled to inform the Raukawa people of her murder. 'Te Puta-a-Ruru' was the place where Ruru came out of hiding. There are variations to this story, but each establishes the relationship of Raukawa, through Ruru and Korekore, to Putāruru and its surrounds. For local authorities, businesses and many of the wider community who actively maintain the morepork version of the town's name, 'home of the owl' provides a more accessible narrative than that of Ruru the ancestor. Conveniently, it also provides a narrative that does not threaten the political autonomy of the local authority, or the powerful economic interests of those who benefit from control and use of the land and resources of the area.

The example of Putāruru is instructive because it illustrates the ease with which Māori narratives and histories connecting people and place have been erased from towns and regions across the country, both physically and figuratively. In this, Putāruru is the norm rather than the exception. As regional New Zealand struggles to carve out a sustainable future in the context of depopulation, structural ageing and shrinking labour forces, towns and centres have much to gain through promoting and leveraging their distinctive identities. Engaging Māori in meaningful partnership through collaboration, co-management and co-production is an essential precursor to reshaping the regions. However, in order for this to happen local authorities need to recognise and provide for mana Māori (Māori autonomy) and mana whenua (territorial rights).

In building this argument we examine the demographic, cultural, political and economic presence of Māori in the regions. We begin with a discussion of the cultural and historical dimensions of Māori place-based attachment with a focus on mana whenua. Mana whenua have responsibilities as kaitiaki (guardians) to the land and resources, to local knowledges and narratives, to iwi and hapū members and to the wider community. The deeply embedded relationships to place and the subsequent responsibilities held by mana whenua make them well placed to champion, and in fact lead, regional revitalisation in Aotearoa.

We next consider the spatial patterning of iwi. Much attention has been given to the high Māori population share in economically deprived areas such as Gisborne and the Far North, but patterns of iwi distribution are poorly understood. This is unfortunate given the growing potential of iwi to contribute to regional sustainability through the process of Treaty-based settlements and development. Our Census-based analysis focuses on the share of iwi members living within their tribal boundaries and finds a great deal of inter-iwi variation. This presents both opportunities and challenges for internal iwi planning and development, but should not be seen in isolation from broader regional trends that include deepening inequality.

A key mechanism for enabling greater Māori engagement in regional development is through local and regional planning and decision-making. While transformative potential is best realised through increased rather than diminished Māori autonomy, there is still a tendency for Māori engagement to be based on token forms of consultation. Despite existing mechanisms and provisions for increased Māori representation and engagement, there have been few best-practice examples where local authorities have actively worked with Māori to transfer decision-making responsibilities. Finally, we provide two case studies, focused on the South Waikato and on Hamilton, to illustrate two very different approaches to recognising mana Māori and mana whenua in the regions.

The enduring and evolving nature of mana whenua

Mana whenua have always derived meaning from place. Mana whenua refers to the mana held by local people who, through whakapapa, have 'demonstrated authority' over land or territory in a particular area. Mana whenua is the localised articulation of what it means to be tangata whenua, and provides for the heterogeneity of experience and expression that tends to be obscured under such umbrella terms as tangata whenua or Māori.

Mana whenua is not the only way of understanding Māori spatiality. There are many place-based concepts that exemplify the enduring nature of place for Māori. Hau kāinga (winds of home/home) and ahi kā (those who maintain occupation/keep the fires burning) are well-known concepts among Māori. Tūrangawaewae, the place where one can stand and belong, is a relatively well-known concept that links people, identity and the land. In the 2013 Māori social survey, Te Kupenga, nearly 70 per cent of Māori reported feeling a 'strong' or 'very strong' connection to tūrangawaewae vis-à-vis their ancestral marae.

Whenua — meaning at once 'land' and 'placenta' — is exemplary in demonstrating the relational and reciprocal arrangements between people and place. This illustrative description is provided by Eva Rickard, who successfully campaigned for the return of ancestral lands at Whaingaroa Harbour to the peoples of Tainui Awhiro:

> First whenua is land. Secondly, whenua is the placenta within the mother that feeds the child before birth. And when it is born this whenua is treated with respect, dignity, and taken to a place in the earth and dedicated to Papatūānuku ... and there it will nurture the child. You know our food and living come from the earth, and there also this whenua of the child stays and says 'this is your little bit of land. No matter where you wander in the world I will be here and at the end of your days you can come back and this is your Papakāinga and this — I will receive you in death' (1977, p. 5).

A perhaps lesser-known concept is that of te ūkaipō — 'the night-feeding breast'. Like tūrangawaewae, this concept establishes a specific place of belonging and nourishment for those who are connected to that place. Ūkaipō is a term that can have dual meaning: referring to one's mother, but also to a specific place where someone can go to gain physical or spiritual sustenance. This is reflected in the instructions, to those who may be living away from their tribal lands or are metaphorically distant, 'e hoki ki tō ūkaipō' — 'return to the night-feeding breast', or to that place where you can go to sustain yourself, recharge and/or regenerate.

For mana whenua, and indeed for those Māori living away from their tribal lands (which, as the next section shows, is the majority of Māori), identity and distinctiveness are inextricably embedded in place. The collective cultural memory of mana whenua is etched into the landscapes and storyscapes of Aotearoa's regions. These storyscapes reference cosmological and social origins, events and encounters, and are enduring. They endure historical and more contemporary colonial impositions; the ebbs and flows of regional population growth or decline; local and central government election cycles, policy development and changes; and economic highs and lows.

As is discussed in the case studies below, these enduring place-based relationships have the potential to provide culturally grounded and transformative approaches to addressing some of the key issues currently facing New Zealand's regions, including environmental protection and economic development that is ethical and sustainable. The challenge lies in local authorities, and the Crown, recognising this and proactively facilitating greater mana whenua participation and autonomy in local and regional planning, management and development. This is not just another opportunity for regions to selectively appropriate those bits of iwi/hapū knowledges that they see as accessible, convenient and useful to their own agenda. While many local authorities have expressed an interest in learning local knowledges, for the most part they have sought to do so on their terms. In so doing, they have failed almost unequivocally in *partnering* with iwi and hapū to lead the revitalisation of their towns and communities in culturally grounded and responsive ways.

Iwi spatiality

Māori have unique forms of place-based attachment that link whānau and whenua, but the extent to which Māori are able to live 'at home' is mediated by structural, historical and political factors. The rural–urban Māori migration that occurred after World War II was one of the most rapid spatial transformations observed for any population anywhere. At the start of the twentieth century, 85 per cent of the Māori population lived in rural locations and 15 per cent in urban locations. By the turn of the century this had reversed, with 85 per cent living in urban settings. These transformations had major implications for rural Māori communities. Some parts of the Hokianga literally emptied out as entire whānau moved to towns and cities. Although aware of their genealogical connections to place, many whānau have lived as mataawaka (outside their own customary rohe, or tribal boundaries) for two or three generations. Contemporary Māori migration has not been confined to Aotearoa New Zealand, with an estimated one in six Māori living overseas, primarily in Australia. At the time of Australia's 2011 Census there were more Māori living in Queensland than in 10 of New Zealand's 16 regional council areas.

Geographical dispersion is an enduring feature of contemporary Māori society and one that is important for iwi and hapū to understand and respond to. However, there are ongoing challenges with accessing information that reflects Māori spatiality and well-being and development priorities. Most administrative boundaries bear little resemblance to customary Māori understandings of rohe. 'Cadastral space' enables planners to demarcate and allocate land-use zones according to development principles and resource management rules. Tribal boundaries are often delineated in relation to landmarks, pou whenua and sometimes key events and ancestors. These boundaries have traditionally been fluid and permeable. For example, the tribal rohe of Raukawa that takes in Putāruru is represented by four pou whenua: Te Pae o Raukawa, Wharepuhunga, Maungatautari and Te Kaokaoroa o Patetere. Tribal kaumātua Haki Thompson described the tribal boundaries of Raukawa as follows:

It [begins] at Te Wairere, from Te Wairere to Tarukenga along Mount Ngongotaha, Tarukenga to Horohoro, from Horohoro to Nukuhau, Nukuhau to Karangahape, from here to Titiraupenga, Titiraupenga to Wharepuhunga, Wharepuhanga to Maungatautari and from Maungatautari back to Te Wairere.

One of the key reasons for undertaking a census is to obtain an accurate count of individuals within a clearly delineated boundary. Subnational population estimates are indispensable for planning and policy-making, and administrative boundaries such as regional councils and territorial authorities (TAs) continue to provide a basis for local-level decision-making. For iwi authorities, knowing how many members live within their rohe is critical. However, obtaining such information is difficult because the spatial classification systems used by Statistics New Zealand do not recognise Māori spatiality in the form of iwi boundaries. For the purpose of this chapter we thus construct our own.

Table 1 shows the proportion of iwi affiliates that resided within their customary rohe at the time of the 2013 Census. In the absence of an official iwi rohe classification, we use Te Kahui Mangai, which identifies the TAs of Mandated and Recognised Iwi Organisations included under the Māori Fisheries Act 2004. In the case of Waikato iwi, for example, this includes the six TAs of Auckland, Waikato, Hamilton City, Matamata Piako, Waipā and Ōtorohanga. This ad hoc approach, which includes entire TAs rather than partial areas, is less than ideal.

Our aggregations are likely to overstate the size of most rohe and, consequently, the proportion of those living inside them. As such, our figures should be taken as generous estimates of within-rohe residence. Table 1 includes 88 of the 110 or so iwi included in the official classification (the rest were not included in Te Kahui Mangai). Here we note that iwi affiliation in the Census is based on self-report, which is quite different from the process of iwi registration. The latter typically requires at least two or three generations of whakapapa to a hapū and/or marae, and some form of external recognition or endorsement by a kaumātua. Iwi register data are the property of iwi and are generally unavailable to researchers.

Table 1: **Proportion of iwi affiliates living within iwi rohe (defined by territorial authority)**

Percentage living within rohe	Percentage of iwi (*n* = 88)
Less than 20%	21.6
20–29.9%	30.7
30–39.9%	21.6
40–49.9%	11.4
Half or more	14.8
Total	100.1

Note: Percentages sum to more than 100 per cent due to rounding

The key point to note from Table 1 is that iwi vary greatly in terms of their within-rohe share. In 2013, only about 15 per cent of iwi had at least half of their members living within reach. Just over half had less than 30 per cent of members living within rohe. And about one in five, including Ngāti Porou (Gisborne), Whakatohea (Ōpōtiki) and Ngāti Maniapoto (Waipā, Ōtorohanga, Waitomo, New Plymouth, Ruapehu), had less than 20 per cent of their peoples living within rohe. The 2013 data closely reflect the distributions in the 2001 Census.

This heterogeneity is not random but reflects, in part, broader structural differences in economic opportunities between and within regions. It is not surprising that the iwi with the highest proportions of within-rohe members are those that incorporate major cities and labour market areas within their boundaries. For example, Ngāti Whātua, Te Kawerau, Ngāti Whanaunga, Waikato, Ngāti Wai, Ngāti Paoa and Ngāti Tamaterā are the iwi with the highest share of within-rohe members. They also include, or are encapsulated within, the Auckland Region.

Iwi have little influence over the structural characteristics of their rohe in terms of population growth, proximity to labour markets, migration flows, structural ageing and (to some extent) economic cycles. Research strongly suggests that income inequality is growing within and between regions. There is also increasing regional divergence in terms of demographic and economic growth, ageing and diversity. As the regions continue to develop unevenly, and inequality perhaps grows, this will almost certainly exact a heavier toll on some iwi than on others.

Enabling effective regional partnerships

Understanding the spatial distribution of iwi and the rohe within which they live can inform and enrich a discussion about the rights and interests of iwi in the planning and development of regions, and subsequent policy responses from central and local government. Historically, the depth and integrity of the latter has been lacking. In 1988, the Waitangi Tribunal reached the conclusion that tino rangatiratanga in the Treaty of Waitangi referred not to separate sovereignty but to tribal self-management in a manner similar to the operation of local government (Muriwhenua Fishing Report). In reality Māori, and tangata whenua in their role as kaitiaki, have struggled to be allowed to make decisions regarding their own affairs and resources at a local level. Local self-government has never eventuated despite a number of provisions and mechanisms for Māori representation in the Local Electoral Act 2001, the Local Government Act 2002 (LGA) and the Resource Management Act 1991 (RMA). Overall, iwi have not been able to obtain an effective level of representation in, and engagement with, local government, or had opportunities for authentic sole governance.

This is partly due to the lack of willingness of local authorities to actively promote forms of Māori representation internally on boards and other decision-making forums. For example, Māori representation in local government has for the past 10–15 years remained static at around 5 per cent, despite Māori accounting for approximately 15 per cent of the population. As we write, the debate about Māori representation on local councils is continuing to be played out in New Plymouth, where the New Plymouth District Council mayor recently resigned after being subjected to blatantly racist attacks because of his support for increased Māori representation on the council.

The absence of Māori authority also reflects inconsistencies in how local authorities engage with iwi on major environmental projects across regions, in spite of their legislative requirement to do so. The RMA intended to provide a high level of public participation, particularly for Māori given their status as tangata whenua and their traditional relationship with natural resources. In reality, Māori are largely excluded from the majority of RMA decision-making processes, with less than 7 per cent of resource consent applications being notified and involving iwi. There are also a number of options and tools available to local authorities to foster iwi decision-making. This includes the ability to transfer RMA powers and functions to iwi authorities under Section 33 of the RMA. However, over the last 25 years, local authorities have been unwilling to transfer these functions or powers.

Since 2005, provision has also existed for Joint Management Agreements (JMAs) as a way of encouraging more collaborative management between councils and Māori. These agreements recognise the status of Māori as tangata whenua and provide potential for Māori to exercise rangatiratanga in relation to natural resources. Despite good intentions, there has been limited use of JMAs outside of Treaty settlements. This is disappointing. The settlement-based co-management agreement and underlying JMAs that were developed for the management of the Waikato River show great potential and demonstrate the benefits of increased representation to iwi and the wider community. The Waikato River Authority, which comprises five iwi and five Crown representatives, has been proactive in attempting to deliver the shared goal of a clean and healthy Waikato River.

It is clear that while a number of mechanisms and provisions exist for Māori representation in and engagement with local government, there are major barriers to implementation. Ultimately, the effectiveness of these provisions and mechanisms will be determined by the willingness of local authorities to fulfil their obligations to Māori and for Māori to be fully supported and empowered in this process.

Building on Arnstein's original ladder of citizen participation, Figure 1 provides a framework for thinking about current and future levels of iwi decision-making and governance, and serves to illustrate that despite there being opportunities for sole governance and representation and engagement with local government, institutional barriers prevent advancement up the ladder and continue to affect economic, cultural, environmental

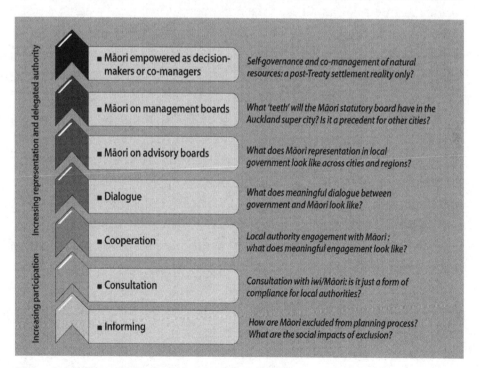

Figure 1: **A ladder of Māori and iwi decision-making**

and social development in the regions. It also presents questions for both iwi and local authorities to consider.

Existing mechanisms for Māori participation, such as those provided for in the RMA and the LGA, fall short of necessitating a Treaty-based relationship between local authorities and iwi and hapū, insofar as the nature and extent of that relationship is a discretionary matter for councils. That being said, we would argue that this necessitates an opportunity for local authorities to show leadership in their engagement with mana whenua to provide bold leadership in regional revitalisation and to demonstrate meaningful and effective Treaty partnerships at the local government level.

While Māori 'development' tends to be framed and responded to at a national level (and, increasingly, iwi level), rangatiratanga is enacted locally. A 'one size fits all' approach cannot address the specific issues, challenges and opportunities that exist within rohe. Formal recognition at a national level does not always lead to improved outcomes at the local level — the inconsistent and weak implementation of the RMA provisions pertaining to Māori is evidence of this.

Mana whenua concepts can help build resilient, sustainable regional development pathways that are also inclusive. To illustrate the potential of these pathways, the next section presents two case studies that address different aspects of mana Māori. The first, located in the South Waikato, presents two important places, Te Wāotū and Te Waihou, that exemplify the challenges and opportunities for mana whenua in terms of building inclusive communities, active protection of significant places and collaborative engagement.

Empowering mana whenua

Case study 1: South Waikato

The Raukawa rohe of Te Kaokaoroa o Patetere, which encompasses much of the South Waikato, contains a number of significant ecological and cultural places that provide the rohe with a distinctive and rich identity. One such example can be found only a short 20 kilometres from Putāruru, in the area known as Te Wāotū. This falls within the traditional lands of the Ngāti Huri hapū, which is now one of the only actively maintained hapū in the area and acts as kaitiaki for a number of other hapū that have traditionally been known to occupy the area. Te Wāotū is the site of one of the first Native Schools in the Waikato, which opened in 1886, and is the standing place of a number of ancestral and ecological sites of significance to hapū and the wider iwi of Raukawa.

This place not only refers to the 'home place' — the tūrangawaewae or ūkaipō — for whānau of Ngāti Huri, but also refers to the physical characteristics of the landscape, the historic standing place of a significant tōtara plantation and the symbolic standing place of a number of ancestral sites. Te Wāotū represents one of many geographically bound concepts that not only serve to define a physical place but also have the potential to provide a hapū-specific conceptual framework for understanding and transforming social, cultural, ecological and political landscapes of the South Waikato. For example, it provides a focal point to collaboratively protect ecologically significant remnants of the native bush at the Jim Barnett Reserve. Further, Te Wāotū has, on numerous occasions, provided a conceptual framework for discussion and engagement between hapū and the community about what it means to stand tall and strong like the historic stand of tōtara.

In addition to the example of Te Wāotū, we can look to the case study of Te Waihou spring to necessitate mana whenua engagement for sustainable regional transformations. Just a short drive out of Putāruru is the Blue Spring, known by mana whenua as Te Waihou. Te Waihou River and its origin as a puna (spring) within the Mamaku range has been a critical part of life for mana whenua for centuries, providing a rich source of both resources and connection. Te Waihou puna is one of a number of significant springs along the Waihou, the water source is a very old groundwater aquifer that sits within the Mamaku/Kaimai area and the quality of the water is exceptional. The spring was, and is, an important resource for the Raukawa hapū of Ngāti Ahuru, Ngāti Tukorehe, Ngāti te Rangi and others as it was located centrally between the marae, and access to the spring and river was shared.

The South Waikato District Council (SWDC), and others, have been quick to capitalise on this distinctiveness. The 2015/16 summer season saw record numbers of visitors to Te Puna Waihou (the Blue Spring), with visible impacts on the puna and its environs. The massive increase in visitor flow was a direct result of the promotion of the spring by the council and others to domestic and international visitors. Along with such promotion and marketing, however, comes the responsibility to ensure that the spring and the surroundings are not negatively affected. The local authority has the opportunity within its Operative District Plan to develop a co-management plan with Raukawa and the Waikato Regional Council for the use and management of Te Puna Waihou. Furthermore, the JMA between SWDC and the Raukawa Settlement Trust, signed in 2013, suggests an emerging era where co-management is a reality rather than just an aspiration. While this may be the case for the Waikato River catchment area, where co-management is a requirement of the Waikato River Settlements, it has yet to be realised in the Waihou catchment and in relation specifically to the Blue Spring.

As well as being a place of extraordinary natural beauty and spiritual significance, Te Waihou has also become a lucrative source of water-generated wealth. Approximately 70 per cent of New Zealand's bottled water is taken from the spring. Water is taken from the municipal supply by the bottling companies without the need for separate resource consents (that would have their own conditions of consent, monitoring and enforcement), for a seemingly nominal fee paid to the local authority. Engagement with mana whenua on this issue has been almost non-existent. The impacts of these commercial water takes stretch far and wide. They include:

— excessive use of water in the production and manufacturing of bottled water, and the other drinks produced by the commercial companies that have 'purchased' rights;
— potential hydrological impacts of water takes on the puna;
— marketing of indigenous places often using information that is questionable;
— the partial privatisation of water (a resource for which access is guaranteed as a fundamental human right); and
— increased pressure on the environment through transportation and packaging of water.

SWDC, in its 2016 annual planning cycle, is now promoting the idea that Putāruru brand itself as the water town. If iwi and hapū are not engaged in the development of a co-management plan for the spring or in the branding of the town, there is a very real chance that history will repeat itself; although rather than perpetuating the myth that Putāruru is the 'home of the owl', the new myth will instead perpetuate symbolic and ecological exploitation of wai Māori (fresh water) — something that is considered by mana whenua to be a taonga (treasure), not a brand.

By the SWDC's own admission in the South Waikato District Plan, engaging with mana whenua and the wider community around the co-management of the Blue Spring is an opportunity for the council to fulfil its obligations to meeting tangata whenua values in the region (Section 3 of the SWDP) and the outstanding natural values of the district (Section 6). The Raukawa Settlement Trust has also articulated its commitment to the spring (and indeed all the waterways in the district) and to engaging with the council through JMAs, numerous submissions to the district and annual planning processes, and in the Raukawa Freshwater Fisheries Plan and the Raukawa Environmental Management Plan (REMP).

We would argue that the opportunity is more than this and is, in fact, one where the council and iwi can lead by example and demonstrate to the community and to others around the country their commitment to proactive management of the spring, and their leadership and innovation in the sustainable management of this place so that it continues to be a distinctive and defining feature of the region. Furthermore, this is an opportunity for the council to step up in a positive way to implement and activate its obligations under the RMA, LGA, SWDP, REMP and, importantly, Te Tiriti o Waitangi. The ability to engage mana whenua in a co-management plan for Te Puna Waihou is entirely possible within the current legislative and policy framework. The willingness on the part of the council to take the lead and partner with iwi and the wider community is yet to be realised, although we are hopeful.

The opportunity for more meaningful partnership between local authorities and iwi is timely, and other examples within the region such as the Waikato River co-management framework demonstrate what is possible if councils and iwi partner to proactively manage this puna. Effective use of the opportunity lies in the willingness of local authorities and the wider community to recognise and actively provide for the distinctiveness of mana whenua relationships to Te Waihou spring. More meaningful engagement and partnerships between council and iwi in relation to the spring can, we believe, see the realisation of new possibilities for resource management, sustainable economic growth, and the creation of a sustainable, distinctive and 'rich' community identity.

Furthermore, in their environmental management plan, Raukawa recognise the opportunities for sustainable economic growth in the district, with Te Waihou spring providing an obvious focal point for attracting people to the area. What is important, they say, is that this can only be done in a context where the natural environment is protected and the values and knowledge of Raukawa upheld. Within this context, with increased mana Māori and partnership in relation to the spring and the wider district, there are many options for meeting the needs of the tribe and the wider community.

In fact, the Raukawa Settlement Trust, which signed its Treaty settlement in 2012, sets out a vision in its 2030 strategic plan — Raukawa Kia Mau Kia Ora — that could equally drive district-wide growth and revitalisation in a way that upholds mana Māori and mana whenua rights and responsibilities as kaitiaki. Raukawa Kia Mau means 'to hold firmly', and speaks of the need to recognise, maintain and actively celebrate the unique identity, traditions and values of Raukawa people and Raukawa whenua (land). Kia Ora means 'to prosper', and represents the idea of growth, sustainable development, and fostering the best opportunities as we move into the future. The iwi is still in the very early stages of post-settlement, and therefore the implementation of this vision is a work in progress; what is clear, though, is that with partnership and increased mana Māori the possibilities could be endless and could apply well beyond the bounds of the resource management sphere.

The point is that mana whenua, in partnership with local authorities and the wider community, should define and determine the specific opportunities and benefits that could come from significant places such as Te Waihou spring. Some examples of what this could look like include sustainable iwi-led or joint ventures that can provide pathways (economic, educational and cultural) for iwi members to 'return home' to the district; the creation of roles for mana whenua that provide employment to protect and maintain the spring (kaitiaki roles); educational programmes about the significance of the spring to the iwi and to the district (beyond simple signage at the spring); and research on and revitalisation of mātauranga Māori and tikanga, or practices and customs, in relation to the spring.

Te Wāotū and Te Waihou are two significant places in the South Waikato that serve to illustrate the opportunities for regions with increased participation by, representation of and partnership with mana whenua at all levels of district and regional decision-making. The challenges and opportunities surrounding Te Waihou are highly relevant, and are still being played out as this chapter is written. Increased recognition, engagement and representation of mana whenua and mana Māori in the South Waikato are opportunities not only to reshape the region but also to exemplify a Treaty partnership in action and, importantly, *with* actions.

Case study 2: Hamilton

While there is a growing awareness of the potential of the 'Māori economy' to contribute to national development, its contribution to regional economies has been largely overlooked, even though in some regions the impact has been substantial. Likewise, the heterogeneity of Māori in regional Aotearoa New Zealand is seldom considered in planning or development.

Hamilton City and its surrounding area provide a useful illustration of both the complexity of contemporary Māori spatiality and the growing economic influence of Māori entities. In Figure 2, the map on the left shows the proportion of the Māori population within the Hamilton main urban area (MUA) that affiliates with the mana whenua iwi of Waikato, Ngāti Maniapoto, Raukawa and Ngāti Hauā. Statistics New Zealand uses the MUA classification to identify concentrated urban or semi-urban settlements without the distortions of administrative boundaries. There are 16 MUAs (12 in the North Island and 4 in the South). The Hamilton MUA encompasses Hamilton City and a number of surrounding towns that form part of a larger commuter zone. The map on the right in Figure 2 shows the spatial distribution of the Māori population (based on descent) as a percentage of the total population in each census area unit (CAU). CAUs are the second-

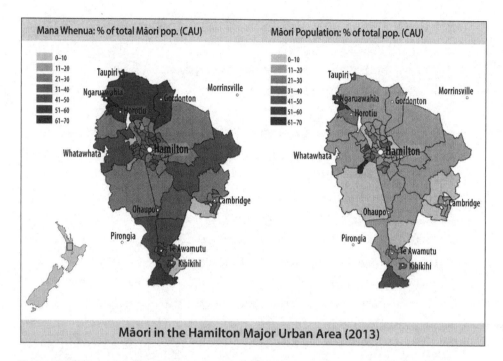

Figure 2: **The spatial distribution of mana whenua and the total Māori population in Hamilton**

smallest unit of dissemination of Census data and are aggregations of meshblocks that often define urban neighbourhoods and suburbs.

In comparison with other cities in Aotearoa New Zealand, Hamilton has a high percentage of mana whenua (38% compared with 16% in Auckland, 6% in Wellington and 29% in Christchurch). However, within the Hamilton MUA the demographic visibility of mana whenua varies substantially, from less than 10 per cent to nearly 70 per cent. High mana whenua concentrations can be found north of Hamilton City in Ngāruawāhia, Horotiu and Gordonton (the urban area excludes Huntly), and to the south of Hamilton City around Te Awamutu and Kihikihi.

This spatial patterning likely reflects the historical clustering of papakāinga communities within proximity of marae, such as Tūranga-waewae in Ngāruawāhia, Hukanui in Gordonton and Mangatoatoa near Kihikihi, as well as connection to ancestral lands where ownership has either been retained or returned to mana whenua. These areas, while in some cases materially disadvantaged, are culturally vibrant focal areas for marae, hapū and iwi development. In more densely populated areas such as Hamilton City, the overall Māori population is concentrated more generally in areas of high socio-economic deprivation (for example, the suburbs of Enderley, Frankton and Glenview).

These maps highlight the ongoing significance of mana whenua connections to place, the demographic importance of mataawaka in urban centres, and the contemporary inequalities that each face. Iwi and urban Māori organisations are well aware of the challenges and opportunities. Māori migration is hardly new, so iwi have had generations to adjust to diasporic flows of whānau outside of the rohe as well as being host to Māori from other parts of the country. How iwi and mataawaka navigate these relationships is informative because it illustrates the potential for constructive engagement and cooperation where competition might otherwise prevail.

Te Rūnanga ō Kirikiriroa is the Urban Māori Authority that represents the needs of mataawaka in Hamilton City, along with Pacific peoples. The rūnanga was established in the mid 1980s under the direction of the late Māori queen, Te Arikinui Te Atairangikaahu, and provides a wide range of services from youth mental health services and budgeting advice to social housing and whānau ora services. The rūnanga explicitly recognises the distinctive rights and interests of mana whenua in Hamilton and seeks to work in ways that complement, rather than compete with, their social, cultural and commercial activities.

Waikato-Tainui, the iwi organisation that covers Hamilton, has about 65,000 registered members from 33 hapū and 68 marae spanning from Te Kuiti in the heart of the King Country to Maraetai in Auckland.

Whakatupuranga 2050, the tribe's long-term strategic blueprint, identifies three key avenues for advancing individual and collective well-being: tribal pride and identity, success in education, and socio-economic independence. Key to the latter is growing the tribe's asset base from the $170 million received in land and cash as part of the Waikato Raupatu Claims Settlement Act 1995.

After difficult beginnings, Waikato-Tainui has become a major economic stakeholder in the region, with the 2015 annual report showing total assets worth $1.2 billion. The portfolio includes four-star hotels; bus operator Go Bus, purchased in a joint venture with Ngāi Tahu Holdings Corporation; and the country's largest shopping complex, The Base. The land on which The Base stands was taken by the Crown under the Public Works Act for defence purposes prior to World War II, and the run-down air force base was returned to the tribe as part of the 1995 settlement. The success of The Base has cemented the tribe's position as a key economic player in Hamilton and contrasts sharply with the struggling retail zone in the city's central business district.

The ubiquity of bilingual signage, which extends to the restrooms and car park, along with the Māori design features and the liberal use of Māori names (the flagship mall is called Te Awa), distinguishes The Base from the other retail centres and malls across the country. It also affirms, in a very direct way, the cultural and symbolic value of te reo and normalises the use of te reo in commercial settings. This contrasts with the (neo)colonial process of predominantly using English place names in the planning and development of commercial and residential sites. The distinctive features of The Base, along with the location of three carved pou, are retained under the terms of the recent 50/50 partnership formed with retailing giant Kiwi Property Group.

Plans by Tainui Group Holdings, the tribe's commercial arm, to build a $3 billion inland port and commercial hub on tribal land near the University of Waikato represent a massive scaling-up from its retail and hotel interests. In so doing, it faces stiff competition from Ports of Auckland, which has entered into a power-play with designs to develop its own freight hub north of Hamilton. If successful, the Waikato-Tainui inland port development will not only diversify the tribe's property-heavy investment portfolio, but will also act as a substantial driver for regional development and greater connectedness in the growth triangle of Auckland, Waikato and the Bay of Plenty.

The relationship between Waikato-Tainui and Hamilton City Council (HCC) over both The Base and the inland port development has at times been stretched. In 2009, HCC developed a variation to its District Plan to restrict further development of The Base. In 2010, Waikato-Tainui disputed the plan change in the High Court, citing that HCC had breached a duty to consult with it as the relevant iwi authority. The presiding judge agreed with Waikato-Tainui. Similarly, in 2013, HCC declined an application for fast-tracking the inland port development. In 2014, at the request of Waikato-Tainui, the Ruakura plan change was heard by the Environmental Protection Authority Board of Inquiry and the plan change was approved. These examples point to some of the issues identified earlier around Māori representation and engagement in the regions. They also highlight the need for local authorities to recognise Waikato-Tainui as both mana whenua and significant resource managers and developers.

In attempting to meet its goals identified in *Whakatupuranga 2050*, Waikato-Tainui will need to create effective and inclusive ways to translate economic success at the collective level to improved well-being for those Waikato-Tainui individuals and whānau in greatest need. This underscores the challenge of balancing responsibilities of manaaki ki te tangata (collective relationships of reciprocity) and tribal capitalism so that existing inequalities are not sharpened in the push to grow collectively owned wealth.

Conclusion

If Aotearoa New Zealand is to capitalise on regional distinctiveness, then this needs to be done in partnership with iwi and hapū, and in ways that recognise and provide for the diversity of mana whenua relationships with place. However, a word of caution is needed. It is not enough to simply 'recognise' iwi and hapū relationships with place — these relationships need to be protected and opportunities for partnerships with mana whenua actively facilitated. Partnership and greater Māori autonomy, we argue, has the potential to create positive, collaborative and innovative strategies for regional revitalisation; much more so than if it is left to a single, territorial political and administrative organisation.

The key spatial transformations that have occurred for iwi mean that a 'one size fits all' approach will not work. In building robust and sustainable regions, one of the most critical and immediate tasks is to ensure that the unique and diverse experiences, knowledges, roles and responsibilities of Māori are respected and acknowledged. The role of local authorities is crucial here in enacting meaningful partnerships with mana whenua and recognising the key role iwi and hapū play in driving change within the regions.

To end we return to Putāruru — a place that, as mentioned already, reflects little of the farming-based and water-generated wealth of the local area. What the town lacks in material wealth, however, is made up for in its richness in community, history and culture, demonstrated through places like Te Wāotū and Te Waihou. This is not always apparent for those passing through on the main highway through town. The challenge lies in generating sustainable growth that attracts to the town those people who want to contribute to the richness of the community and not extract or exploit it for their own individual purposes. Mana whenua understand the importance of the collective to the well-being of the town and wider region. This means that the role and responsibility of iwi and hapū, in this area, are multiple, and involve advocating and caring for iwi members; proactively seeking opportunities to facilitate the return of iwi members to their ahi kaa/tūrangawawewae/ūkaipō; fostering relationships with the wider community; and establishing connections and relationships with new and diverse members of the community within an ethics of manaakitanga (hospitality) and whanaungatanga (relationship-building).

It is time to recognise in a meaningful way the distinctive, rich and innovative histories and solutions that mana whenua and mana Māori provide our communities, beyond the simplistic and convenient narratives such as 'home of the owl'. Mana whenua have a compelling reason to champion the revitalisation of the South Waikato, and indeed of New Zealand's regions: our collective identity is embedded in the land. While individuals move, tangata whenua are here to stay and have intergenerational responsibilities as mana whenua and as kaitiaki. The role of mana whenua in reshaping the regions has never been more important.

The authors acknowledge the support provided by the MBIE research grant, Capturing the Diversity Dividend in Aotearoa New Zealand (CaDDANZ), and the University of Waikato Faculty of Arts and Social Sciences Contestable Research Fund.

References

Arnstein, Sherry R. (1969). A ladder of citizen participation. *Journal of the American Institute of Planners, 35 (4),*: 216–224.

Rickard, E. (1977). Whenua. In B. Gadd (ed.), *Pacific Voices: An anthology of writing by and about Pacific people.* Albany: Stockton House.

4.

Down on main street:

The depopulation of the central North Island

Alice Kranenburg
Whakatāne District Council

Down on main street: The depopulation of the central North Island

In the context of urban or rural population the terms 'decline' or 'shrinkage' carry negative connotations. We have a natural anxiety about decline, and there are few positive narratives. A common reaction is try to 'solve the problem' of decline. This can be partly attributed to the unwavering focus of planning theory and practice on growth as a planning paradigm. The stigma attached to the term 'decline' leads to the perception that something needs to be fixed. Society tends to stress the merits of growth — if it is not occurring, then something must be wrong. These perceptions can have direct impacts on regional investment and community pride.

Research, both nationally and internationally, tends to focus on ways of dealing with growth; there has been far less research carried out on the process of planning for declining populations. As many rural New Zealand districts experience only minor population growth, or population decreases, district councils are faced with the task of continuing to provide acceptable services with a dwindling ratepayer base. Additionally, these areas are typically lower on the socio-economic scale, and their existing ratepayer base is often financially limited.

It is extremely difficult to address decline on a political level. Local governments are accustomed to planning for growth, including increases in population and job opportunities; they are much less equipped to cope with decline. The democratic nature of local government also works against this type of planning; planning for shrinkage can be the equivalent of political suicide. Instead of accepting decline, politicians tend to try to manage it with plans for revitalisation. Against this backdrop of a growth-oriented planning culture, many cities and districts cannot accept that they are in decline. Further, population decline is self-reinforcing, tending to provoke changes in the living environment, which in turn lead to further population decline.

The closure of a factory or mill by the dominant employer in an area can spark the first steps in the process of rural-to-urban migration as workers leave to find jobs elsewhere. And when those workers are young people, the impact is exacerbated. This is symptomatic of wider economic changes in the country since the economic reforms of the mid 1980s; the centralisation of services, particularly government departments, has had a profoundly negative impact on employment opportunities in regional New Zealand.

Planning for decline requires a total change in the thinking of local government, residents and other stakeholders. Some services may be eliminated in this process; others will be developed further in order to provide for the affected community. For example, some local authorities are investigating the idea of asking new businesses moving to their district to go 'off the grid' in terms of stormwater, wastewater and electricity services. A small number of districts have accepted the reality of decline, and these areas have already started developing 'smart shrinkage' strategies. Smart decline is planning for less: fewer people, fewer buildings and reduced land use.

In an urban context, decline produces its own fundamental set of issues and challenges, the most prevalent of which relates to governance, which becomes complicated as a result of the multitude of stakeholders and actors involved. The mobilisation of resources is crucial to shrinking cities, and the decisions made by politicians, local enterprises and representatives from civil society can lead to alternative governance arrangements which play a huge role in steering decline. As a city declines in population, its financial capability is reduced and it becomes far more difficult to maintain the level of service previously provided.

In a rural context such as New Zealand's there are four categories: rural areas with high urban influence, rural areas with moderate urban influence, rural areas with low urban influence, and highly rural/remote areas.

Small towns are typically neglected in political and academic discourses, even though they are a key part of the rural economy, possibly because of a perception that their contribution to overall gross domestic product (GDP) is significantly lower than that of primary producers such as farmers. Political understanding and processes have a significant influence on the development of small towns, which are key players in terms of development opportunities. The sense of community within smaller towns is another resource; communities in decline typically contain significant numbers of lifetime residents, who can enhance the social capital of the area. Indeed, rather than looking to traditional economic and population indicators, criteria such as social and environmental stability can be much more effective in determining the overall vitality of a small community.

Decline need not be a terminal, or an entirely undesirable, condition. Yes, managing population decline can be an essentially pessimistic task, but there are also opportunities, including building resilience in communities, urban renewal, high rates of institution-initiated community engagement, adjustment to 'planning for less', and the development of new tools for planning for decline.

Areas of decline typically demonstrate higher rates of participation by the community in the planning process. Compared with growing communities, they show higher rates of civic and community involvement, and the length of time individuals have resided in an area has a direct positive effect on the level of their social and community involvement. There is some speculation that this higher level of involvement stems from a sense of obligation. However, there is little evidence to support this argument; the main driver for a higher rate of community participation seems to be the desire of residents to give back to their community. Other positive symptoms of decline include increased housing affordability, access to natural amenities, little or no traffic congestion, and low pollution levels that stem from a lack of growth pressures in the area. A slower pace of life is a further benefit. The importance of these characteristics lies in the sense of 'place' that they engender, something that may not be found in growing cities.

Local identity, governance practices and other local features will determine the manner in which declining communities react to external pressures, reflecting the pressure and importance of social capital, which includes attitudes, relationships, institutions and values that govern interactions between people and which contributes to economic and social development.

Community involvement is a highly significant resource when it comes to addressing and living with decline. Local identity feeds into community involvement: the greater the identification of the local population with their town, the greater their interest in supporting local initiatives.

Planning for population decline could be considered to be a thankless task. However, it also provides the opportunity for urban or community renewal. To effectively address the issue of decline, regional strategies must utilise investment well and make the best use of available public funding and technical and social infrastructure.

However, the question still remains: How *do* we plan for decline? New Zealand has no explicit policies for dealing with it. The situation is the same in most other countries, with a very modest literature outlining specific instances of policy that addresses decline. But it's not just about planning tools; a new way of thinking about places and communities is needed.

Ruapehu: a case study in decline

Ruapehu District, in the central North Island, has much in common with many other rural districts across New Zealand. For instance, a high proportion of the local economic activity is based on agriculture. The majority of the areas in the district can be classed as rural areas with low urban influence, with some parts falling into the category of highly rural/ remote areas.

Ruapehu was one of the last parts of New Zealand to be settled by Europeans, owing to the remoteness of the district and Māori resistance towards the end of the Land Wars. Mount Ruapehu is part of the district, as is a large part of the Tongariro National Park, and the district has two main centres, Taumarunui (2274 residents at the 2013 Census) and Ohakune (987), and six other small towns: National Park (171), Ohura (129), Owhango (174), Raetihi (1002), Raurimu (534), and Waiouru (738). The town centres are predominantly surrounded by productive land, including sheep and beef farms, farms growing vegetables (such as carrots) and some dairy farms. The district has good freight connectivity to regional hubs that include Hamilton and Palmerston North and which are of importance to primary producers in the area.

It is a picturesque part of New Zealand, but it is affected by a number of issues that have contributed to a pattern of decline over the past few decades. Between the 2006 and 2013 censuses, the total permanent population of the Ruapehu District dropped from 13,569 to 11,844, a decline of 12.7 per cent over the seven years, the highest rate of decline in New Zealand at the time.

Although resident numbers are continuing to fall, there has also been an increase in tourist visits throughout the district, particularly in the summer months. Since mid 2012, there has been a noticeable increase in tourism spending in the district, primarily because of new cycle trails, including the Timber Trail through the central North Island and the

Mountains to Sea Trail through the Ruapehu and Whanganui districts.

When I conducted key informant interviews with both staff and elected representatives at the Ruapehu District Council to understand the everyday practices of planning for local decline, I discovered that several factors contribute to the current situation in the district, a key being health care. Like many other funding mechanisms, district health board funding is allocated on a population basis, a formula that often fails to account for factors such as isolation and the inability to physically reach health-care facilities. As a result the district struggles to attract good medical professionals.

Another significant factor is education, and this has had a major impact on retaining skilled young people. The Ruapehu District has 21 primary schools but only two secondary schools (Ruapehu College and Taumarunui High School). With such a limited choice, parents who are able to do so often send their children to boarding schools in Hamilton. Many of the local schools face similar issues to the medical centres — attracting teachers to the district can be a significant challenge because of its remoteness and being an area of poverty and high crime. Ruapehu District also has a significant divide between the district's north and south; indeed, each area has its own iwi and distinctive set of communities. As a result it is difficult to establish cohesion and a shared vision.

The largest sources of employment in Ruapehu are agriculture, tourism and government. Sheep and beef farming provide a significant proportion of the agricultural jobs, followed by farm support services. However, jobs in agriculture within the district have become more scarce at a rate of 20 per cent over the past decade. Tourism jobs in the district are related to the ski fields and, more recently, the cycle trails. The government sector includes defence, health care and education; however, jobs in this sector have also been shrinking. In addition, there are two significant industrial sectors: heavy and civil engineering, and pulp, paper and board manufacturing

(Winstone International operates a plant at Tangiwai). Both of these are declining sharply, and their skilled employees predominantly fly in and out of the district.

Social deprivation is a significant issue in the district. According to the Social Deprivation Index — which indicates areas suffering from a combination of significant negative social factors, including a lack of internet access, a high proportion of people receiving a benefit, high levels of unemployment, and little access to transport — the district's top three most deprived areas are Ohura village, Taumarunui and Raetihi.

All signs point towards the continuation of population decline in the district. Young people are migrating from the district to major urban centres, leaving the aged and unskilled behind. Some leave to pursue tertiary education, and although some say they would like to return to Ruapehu, the lack of opportunities for skilled individuals prevents them from doing so. The loss of young people changes the population structure, and there are other flow-on effects, too: the need for schooling drops and the need for aged care increases. And, as the district's resident population continues to fall, so does the rating base.

The tone of the interviews I conducted was generally one of resolve. The key informants all accepted that population decline was a significant feature of their district's recent history, although there were some differences in the level of acceptance in terms of the future and the possibility of 'reversing' this trend. All those I spoke to shared a level of determination and the common goal of enhancing the district for its residents. However, I also noticed some differences in expectations, ranging from complete acceptance of the realities (such as the likelihood of no growth for the foreseeable future) to instances of denial (such as talk of how to reverse the population decline). These divergent views of the district's future could affect the success of council-led measures to plan for decline, and could also have an impact on the community's perception of what it means to be a citizen in a declining area.

The decline in the population and the rating base has had many flow-on effects throughout the district, including infrastructure cost-sharing and key health-care and education issues. In the Ruapehu District a strategy of service withdrawal is largely impossible because much of the existing infrastructure caters for a far greater number of people than live in the area, as a result of the numbers of temporary visitors and tourists. However, population numbers are used to calculate central government funding in areas such as roading, health and education services, and so with population numbers falling it is difficult for the Ruapheu District Council to continue to attract the same level of funding.

Infrastructure cost-sharing is a significant burden on ratepayers. The cost of maintaining the existing infrastructure in the district continues to rise as standards are continually upgraded. The Ruapehu District Council spends almost half of its budget on roading, and adjusted funding assistance rates from the New Zealand Transport Agency ensure that this burden doesn't fall too heavily on ratepayers. 'Low volume, rural networks have the potential to be expensive for residents,' says the council's economic development manager Warren Furner, 'so building credibility and advocating at a central government level are key to having an affordable roading network.'

On a positive note, a number of opportunities have also emerged from Ruapehu's population decline. The council has taken on the role of economic development facilitator for the district, an unusual decision given that territorial authorities do not typically assume this responsibility. Some residents opposed this decision; they felt that it was not part of the council's core functions. But the council felt that in order to carry out effective long-term planning, it needed to know what type of future it should be planning for.

In an urban environment decline can spark renewal opportunities:

the reuse of vacant buildings, downsizing and demolition can, for example, form part of a wider urban redevelopment scheme. The Ruapehu District Council is using population decline as an opportunity to carry out some much-needed urban regeneration of particular spaces, including the main street of Taumarunui, where a number of business have closed, leaving empty buildings behind. The street is very long, and the remaining businesses are spread along it rather than being consolidated into one vibrant area.

Although the council has asked the people of Taumarunui for their vision for the future of their central business area, the approach being taken with this project is still very much top-down. Residents were initially reluctant to accept the rather drastic changes proposed for their town centre, and some felt that the council had stepped outside its role. But it's clear that dealing with empty shops is a significant challenge for the proposed town-centre revitalisations. One option suggested was to 'pull them down, and make them into green spaces'; the practical means of achieving this was not elaborated on. 'It's very difficult in declining communities to implement urban design protocols, due to locals feeling like they are losing their history,' Mayor Don Cameron told me. 'But we want to create spaces that are interesting, and that people will appreciate.'

One idea that has resonated with the communities in Ruapehu is meaningful community engagement — not only in the planning process but also in the management of assets and the allocation of funding. The very high level of citizen involvement in the Ruapehu District is demonstrated by the river valley funding scheme, in which funds were set aside for a group of rural roads within 10 river valleys. Council roading staff held discussions with farmers and residents to best determine which road works needed prioritising, and the active engagement with those affected made a significant contribution to the final decision. 'It is about having a conversation,' the mayor explained. 'And from that, councillors require it to be a part of the standard process.'

A sector that has grown for Ruapehu, but would not necessarily grow in all declining areas, is tourism. The increase in visitor numbers has boosted economic activity in the district, thereby saving a number of struggling businesses. The area has always been a winter destination, particularly Ohakune and National Park, which are the gateways to the Turoa and Whakapapa ski fields, respectively, and more recently, visitor numbers have also increased during the warmer months following the establishment of the cycle trails. As a result, the district is now a year-round destination for tourists.

One of the most significant direct impacts of continuing population decline is the difficulty of fostering resilience in communities. Resilience can be defined as the ability of a community to adapt to and shape change, and the development of resilience becomes more challenging if there is a lack of 'good young people' to undertake projects and bring in new ideas. In the past decade this has been an important issue for Ruapehu given that a lack of community participation by young people of the previous generation has affected the cohesion of the wider community.

Government support and outside investment is becoming increasingly important to regional New Zealand, and the economic focus on the main centres is having a negative impact on the rest of the country. Many regions are based on primary industries such as dairy, sheep and beef production; without support from central government during price troughs, rural regions are almost completely at the mercy of international commodity prices. The Ruapehu District has been affected by falling wool, sheep and beef prices during the past two decades and has also felt the recent drop in dairy prices. The council is under pressure to provide services to its community at the same level as previously, but diversification and new business start-ups are seen as too risky to try in regional New Zealand, which leaves a very limited range of options for any attempt at growth.

Support from central government, potentially in some form of regional development strategy and incentives, as was used during the 1970s to encourage industries to move into the regions, would be welcomed, not only to bolster regional economies but also to take pressure off Auckland's frantic growth. Other countries experiencing rural decline, such as Germany, provide rural regions with central government assistance. But, on a political level, the challenge of planning for decline can be immense. An additional issue for the Ruapehu District is that expenditure on infrastructure consumes the majority of the district's budget, and this is not always reflected in the value of the infrastructure. The key example is roading; the degree to which roading through the Ruapehu District contributes to exports on a national scale needs to be better reflected in the financial support provided by central government for that roading.

Attracting outside investment is another avenue for economic development of the district that was stressed by the interviewees. The quality of the secondary schools and health-care services is key to this but both these services are outside the scope of council influence, which has led the council to implement other means to achieve this goal. The district's Economic Development Strategy, released in June 2015, was written with comprehensive community involvement and provides a platform for the Ruapehu District to explore different mechanisms that may contribute to the district's economic profile.

One of the drivers is the recognition that there is no single solution to issues such as economic development in association with decline. The danger inherent in creating this type of strategy, of course, is that the Ruapehu District Council could be trying to 'fix the problem' of decline. However, the strategy also contains elements that could be considered to be ways of planning for smart decline. While the Economic Development

Strategy ultimately aims to attract new business to the district, it also focuses on enabling existing businesses to succeed by 'cutting red tape' — making it easier for businesses to deal with the council, enabling them to spend time and money on improving their business rather than on complying with council regulations, for example. Deregulation can be a useful tool in planning for smart decline because it focuses both on supporting existing businesses and on attracting new ones.

Tourism was also identified in the interviews and in the Economic Development Strategy as a key element of the district's economic profile. The Ruapehu District Council is pushing for the area to become an all-year-round destination. It is important, however, that increased visitor numbers are not seen as the 'silver bullet' for economic issues within the district.

Urban renewal has positive implications for the Ruapehu District, and is one of the proposals put forward as part of the Economic Development Strategy. The opportunity to review a town's urban form, and analyse what makes spaces within towns liveable, is one of the more positive processes arising from planning for decline. In the case of the Taumarunui main street, the recognition that the currently empty shops will not be filled is a sign of acceptance, a response that's fundamental to effective planning for smart decline.

Another positive part of urban renewal is the opportunity for more extensive engagement. Council-initiated community engagement, whether it be a town-centre redesign or the funding allocation for land transport projects, is widely regarded as best practice for local government entities. There have been positive outcomes, both for the council and for the community, from this engagement. But there are, naturally, also some risks. One is the danger of 'consultation fatigue', where members of the public simply have too many strategies, plans and policies to read and comment on and thereby lose interest in, or gloss over, issues that directly affect them. While there is no evidence of this having occurred in Ruapehu, it is undoubtedly something to be aware of.

Conclusion

The processes that have contributed to the Ruapehu District's population decline reflect a growing reality for many rural and regional areas in New Zealand. Population decline in the Ruapehu District highlights a range of complex economic and social factors, and the challenge of explicitly addressing decline. The challenge of funding infrastructure in a district that is sparsely populated with a number of isolated communities is significant, and a point of contention in terms of support from central government. Economic development facilitation by the district council, and the importance of external investment, both stem from the inadequacy of the central government's current role in regional New Zealand. However, the research also revealed a specific set of opportunities for the Ruapehu District. The chance to reshape urban spaces that have seen dramatic changes in community composition, and engaging the community to take part in decision-making alongside the council, are key elements that will provide new opportunities. There are also significant, although somewhat unpredictable, opportunities stemming from the thriving tourism sector.

Decline as a fundamental concept is inherently complex, with incomplete, contradictory and changing factors that can often be difficult to recognise — let alone address. This complexity makes the question of how the Ruapehu District Council (or indeed much of regional New Zealand) can plan for population decline very challenging to answer.

5. No region left behind:
Local success stories in regional innovation

Christine Cheyne
Massey University

No region left behind: Local success stories in regional innovation

In his 2016 State of the Nation address, Prime Minister John Key asserted that '[e]very region of New Zealand is crucial to our growth and progress'. He then went on to say, in what appeared to be a qualification of this, 'But on New Zealand's behalf, Auckland is competing with Asia-Pacific's great global cities. It's our version of Sydney, Singapore or Shanghai.' The growth of the Auckland region was portrayed as being in the national interest.

In orthodox economics, the measure of growth is any increase in per capita income; it may also be measured by growth in population, which is often associated with growth in per capita income. However, the costs of economic growth are not accounted for because New Zealand lacks a comprehensive measure of the economic impact of Auckland's growth. A critical question that needs to be addressed is: What are the implications of growth in one area for other areas?

In view of the prime minister's assertion that every region is crucial to national growth and progress, this chapter looks at some examples of regional innovation outside the Auckland region and considers what local government and economic development agencies need to do in order to enhance regional innovation at the subnational level. The chapter begins by briefly reviewing the role of local government in economic development and identifying some of the economic development agencies that exist at the subnational level. Some contemporary examples of regional innovation are highlighted. Drawing on these examples, the chapter concludes with a brief outline of some factors that are critical for enhanced regional innovation.

The role of local government in economic development

From its beginnings in the mid nineteenth century following the establish-ment of settler government in New Zealand, local government has had a role in economic development. The newly established municipalities initially focused on infrastructure such as roads, water, gas supply, street lighting and drainage, which were critical to local economic development. It was not until 1989 that local government legislation articulated the purpose of local government. As Professor Graham Bush has commented, the new section added in 1989 to the Local Government Act 1974 effectively asserted that New Zealand comprised 'different communities with differing needs and that local government provides a means whereby those affected can actively determine the nature and meeting of those needs' (Bush, 1995, pp. 125–6).

Around the same time, the then Local Government Association had sought to define the core functions of local government, one of which was 'development and promotion' of the area (Bush, 1995, p. 128). Several years later, Bush observed that the primary areas of local government involvement in economic development were acquisition of land and buildings, and promotion of the local economy, sister cities and tourism. Tensions were often present, arising in part from the uncertainty of funding sources and, related to this, in part from resistance from ratepayers to local government venturing beyond its more conventional roles such as providing roads, safeguarding public health and other specific roles prescribed by legislation (Bush, 1995, p. 128).

In 2002, new legislation was enacted that specifically recognised local government's role in economic well-being. The Local Government Act 2002 (LGA 2002) was a broadly empowering statute which stated that a purpose of local government was to 'promote the social, economic, environmental, and cultural well-being of communities, in the present and for the future'. This applied to both regional councils and territorial authorities (city/

district councils). From 2002, local government consolidated its important and long-standing role in economic development.

In December 2012, however, amendments to the LGA 2002 removed the statutory purpose that had been in place for a decade, and instead the act now states that a purpose of local government is to 'meet the current and future needs of communities for good-quality local infrastructure, local public services, and performance of regulatory functions in a way that is most cost-effective for households and businesses'. This was an attempt to constrain local government, but the other key element in the purpose of local government remains unchanged: namely, 'to enable local democratic decision-making and action by, and on behalf of, communities'. Thus, local government in New Zealand retains a degree of autonomy through its electoral accountability not to central government but to local communities and through its degree of financial independence.

Despite the legislative amendments in 2012, local government has not radically reduced its role in economic development and, indeed, the emphasis on meeting the current and future needs of communities for good-quality local infrastructure and local public services implicitly, if not explicitly, recognises the broad role of local government in activities connected to economic development. As Table 1 shows, economic development is a key area of expenditure by local government.

When the Auckland Council was created in 2009, central government's intention was to strengthen regional leadership and coordinated regional planning. The legislation specifically requires the mayor of Auckland to 'articulate and promote a vision for Auckland'. Section 79 of the Local Government (Auckland Council) Act 2009 requires the Auckland Council to develop a spatial plan for Auckland, the purpose of which is 'to contribute to Auckland's social, economic, environmental, and cultural well-being through a comprehensive and effective long-term (20- to 30-year) strategy for Auckland's growth and development'. The leadership

Table 1: **Local Authority Financial Statistics**
Total operating expenditure by activity

	2012	2013	2014	2015
Roading	1,361,785	1,407,194	1,401,972	1,448,459
Transportation	1,073,412	995,722	949,099	1,041,119
Water supply	443,392	405,995	437,014	520,115
Wastewater	738,751	755,157	769,980	751,599
Solid waste/refuse	304,452	269,850	304,780	355,002
Culture	293,671	311,685	292,810	338,859
Recreation & sport	497,998	460,268	480,016	561,734
Environmental protection	651,301	704,774	811,378	873,478
Planning and regulation	318,810	325,946	305,092	343,955
Property	39,970	39,420	38,276	42,235
Emergency management	501,765	440,168	488,623	645,634
Community development	170,034	192,195	189,814	203,126
Economic development	252,174	244,486	267,823	290,810
Governance	189,975	132,367	177,189	216,316
Council support services	1,244,031	1,225,454	1,301,334	1,154,682
Other activities	302,954	290,494	171,488	156,900
Total	8,384,475	8,201,175	8,386,688	8,944,023

Source: Statistics New Zealand (2016)

role of local government is clearly recognised.

At the time of Auckland Council's establishment, the legislation mandated the creation of a number of council-controlled organisations (CCOs), arms-length organisations that are accountable to the parent council through a Statement of Intent. One of these CCOs, Auckland Tourism, Events and Economic Development Limited (ATEED), specifically focuses on economic development, with the goals of lifting the Auckland region's economic well-being, and supporting and enhancing the ability of the region to compete internationally. It does this by identifying new opportunities for economic growth and developing strategies to achieve this growth. For example, a recent initiative of ATEED is to develop a strategy for Auckland to be a global centre of sports training, innovation, science and medicine, a sector that in recent years has had annual global growth of more than 10 per cent.

Together, these three aspects of the Auckland Council — first, the statutory requirement to carry out spatial planning that is focused on economic and social development (as distinct from the unitary plan, which is concerned with land use); second, the requirement for the mayor to articulate a vision and the associated powers; and third, central government's requirement for economic development to be handled by a CCO — affirm the role of local government in economic development at the regional level. Other councils in New Zealand are not governed by the same legislation: mayors outside Auckland do not have the same powers as the Auckland mayor and nor is there a requirement to carry out spatial planning or to have a CCO focused on economic development. Nevertheless, there is considerable involvement in economic development by both regional councils and territorial authorities.

Local Government New Zealand (LGNZ), the peak body for the local government sector, has had a work programme in place since 2010 that highlights local government's vital role in and contribution to New

Zealand's economic growth. A key goal for LGNZ is to address economic prosperity and growth across the country and to demonstrate how local government, central government and businesses can work together to achieve this. A particular challenge is the very uneven regional growth that has recently been experienced. Regional economic performance has proved to be very volatile and the drivers are very complex (Eaqub & Stephenson, 2014).

This volatility and complexity, however, shows that simplistic assumptions about the growth or decline of regions are likely to be unreliable. Declining regions can recover and growth can be halted. Local political leaders and local councils play a vital role in identifying opportunities for increased prosperity built on the unique strengths of their district/region and their natural resources, infrastructure and people. They also have a key role in promoting their district/region.

Local government's role in economic development has been actively supported by central government, in recognition of the important local and regional leadership role of local government. For example, in mid 2014 the Ministry of Business, Innovation and Employment (MBIE) and Ministry for Primary Industries (MPI) jointly launched the Regional Growth Programme for working with businesses, iwi and Māori, and councils to identify growth opportunities in selected regions. Indeed, MBIE considers that its role is to assist key cities and regions that have particular needs. Its website states that its role is to 'provide advice that helps maximise the contribution that regions and cities make to NZ's economic development and prosperity. This includes a focus on regions facing long-standing challenges, and our key cities of Auckland and Christchurch.'[1] In the first two years, the focus has been on five regions.[2] The key component of the programme is the

──────

1   See http://www.mbie.govt.nz/info-services/sectors-industries/regions-cities.

2   Tai Tokerau/Northland, Bay of Plenty, East Coast (Gisborne and Hawke's Bay), Manawatū-Whanganui and West Coast.

commissioning of a series of in-depth regional growth studies to be carried out by independent consultants to inform and influence a range of private-sector and public-sector investments, plans and strategies.

Long before the Regional Growth Programme, collaboration between councils and local industries and other stakeholders has been evident in many regions. Most, if not all, regional councils and other city and district councils have developed economic development strategies for their district or region. Many councils contribute to non-governmental organisations that receive funding from industry as well (such as Venture Taranaki and Venture Southland, discussed below). Local political leaders have developed networks for promoting economic development, including mayoral forums such as the Waikato Mayoral Forum and the national organisation, the Mayors Taskforce for Jobs.

Recognition of the integrated nature of economic, social and environmental well-being has meant that despite the December 2012 legislative change by central government, local government leaders and managers cannot and should not significantly scale back involvement in local and regional economic development. Even regional councils, which focus primarily on environmental quality and natural resource management, consider that they have a role in promoting and providing for regionally significant services, amenities and infrastructure and representing their region's interests and contributions to the regional, national and international community.

Innovations in regions outside Auckland

In the space of a brief chapter it is not possible to comprehensively review regional innovations. Here the focus is on a few examples that have been effective over a longer time-frame and that have developed a successful structure and approach to economic development.

Venture Southland, the agency responsible for the Southland region's economic and community development initiatives, was established in July 2001 and is funded by the Invercargill City, Southland District and Gore District councils and the Community Trust of Southland. Governance is by a joint committee made up of elected and community representatives from the three councils. The joint committee meets monthly and its agendas and minutes are publicly available. A distinctive feature is that Venture Southland has an explicit focus on both economic and community development. Monitoring and an overview of activities is provided by an advisory subcommittee comprising the three Southland mayors and one iwi representative. An annual Venture Southland action plan is prepared in accordance with the Strategy for Development 2006–2016. Accountability is reported through Venture Southland's statement of service performance, annual accounts and audit report. An annual publication, the *Year in Review*, publicises Southland success stories and a summary of the financial statements to complement the annual financial statements.

Venture Southland's focus has been on retaining and attracting skilled labour and diversifying the economy. The Southland Workforce Strategy 2014–2031 was completed in 2015, and implementation of the strategy is now the focus. Specific initiatives address youth pathways to employment. Alleviating labour force challenges through business efficiency was a focus in 2015, with seven businesses completing the Lean Manufacturing programme and 10 dairy farms completing the Dairy Lean programme. Highlighting the success of this innovation by Venture Southland, DairyNZ adopted the Venture Southland Dairy Lean model for a nationwide roll-out starting in Canterbury and Waikato in 2016.

Venture Southland's Business team facilitated the Regional Business Partnership, which secured $200,000 in funding on a matched basis from New Zealand Trade and Enterprise and an additional $150,000 in research and development funding from Callaghan Innovation (a government agency supporting high-tech businesses in New Zealand).

Diversification of Southland's economy is a key goal of Venture Southland. Work has been undertaken, as part of a regional high-value-foods project, on developing a business case for potential investors. Tourism is another area of focus for diversifying the economy, with significant growth predicted at a national level (Venture Southland, 2015).

One particularly notable example of successful regional entre-preneurialism that is nationally — indeed internationally — significant is the Awarua Satellite Tracking Station in Southland. This is a small space base that was initially used by the European Space Agency to monitor resupply missions to the International Space Station. More recently it became linked with a new project involved in photographing the entire planet every day. A fleet of satellites transmit the pictures back to ground stations on Earth, including one on farmland at Awarua, chosen for its remote location and lack of radio interference. As the project manager has pointed out, 'A lot of the spacecraft go over the poles, and the further south you are the better . . . So clearly Southland's got an advantage over anywhere else in New Zealand.'

This regional example shows how technological innovation over-comes (or perhaps depends on and exploits) geographical distance and remoteness. However, what was important was the human capital (such as Venture Southland's funding of an enterprise project manager position) and the initial funding for the investment in infrastructure. In 2015, the project received increased attention with two new operators operating from the Awarua site.

Venture Taranaki, Taranaki's regional development agency, like Venture Southland, is a trust funded primarily by local government. Its vision is to help businesses grow and prosper, and to grow the visitor industry and global brand of Taranaki through teams that focus on different aspects: economic development, tourism, marketing and events. Venture Taranaki works one-on-one with individuals, businesses, small groups, media and industry sectors. The main source of funding is New Plymouth District Council, but there is also support from the Stratford and South Taranaki district councils, Taranaki Electricity Trust, TSB Community Trust, New Zealand Trade and Enterprise, Callaghan Innovation, Business Mentors New Zealand and many other private-sector organisations. The agency provides resources and toolkits for businesses and prospective businesses and also assists with inward investment into the region.

Geographical location is, to some extent, a challenge for the region, though less so than it is for Southland. Taranaki has historically had a boom–bust economy associated with its traditional industries of oil/gas and dairying. Both industries have recently experienced a sudden and increasingly severe downturn, prompting regional innovation. Venture Taranaki has been involved in infrastructural development projects that include broadband, roading and the port. Transport infrastructure and regional branding are critical for the region to be able to diversify from its traditional industrial base.

As in Southland, tourism has considerable potential, given the coastal location, Egmont National Park and other natural assets. To increase the resilience of the agricultural sector, Venture Taranaki is involved in two significant 'agri-opportunity' projects: one associated with industrial hemp and another with mānuka honey. Massey University has recently conducted a research project into the benefits of growing industrial hemp (*Cannabis sativa*) as a commercial crop in Taranaki. Internationally, the crop is regarded as having enormous potential to deliver economic and environmental benefits. An Agribusiness Innovation Grant was obtained from the New Zealand Agricultural and Marketing Research and Development Trust and support was also provided by Venture Taranaki, Taranaki Regional Council, Hemp Technologies Ltd and others for a study of the application and benefits of growing industrial hemp and to identify the pathways to its cultivation as a non-food-chain commercial end-product (fibre), while also improving the quality of land-farmed soils. Growing conditions in Taranaki are ideal and there is also increasing world demand. As well as the economic return to farmers, there is the potential for employment creation associated with processing of the raw material.

Building on research undertaken in 2014 in conjunction with Lincoln University on the opportunities associated with mānuka honey, Venture Taranaki also organised a national mānuka conference in early 2016 to provide more information to those interested in entering the mānuka industry. Growth of this industry is part of MPI's challenge to the primary sector to double exports by 2025 (a goal that may be achieved within a much shorter time-frame).

Fostering regional innovation

Regional innovation led by local government working in conjunction with iwi, business, central government and other key stakeholders is clearly capable of delivering economic prosperity and reducing uneven regional development. It requires support and resourcing (in particular, research and funding) from central government. Planning for the shift to service-sector economies and harnessing opportunities associated with technological change are critical for regional economic development. MBIE's Regional Growth Programme is a tentative start to providing the necessary support for regions from the centre. Its focus is on identifying current regional sectoral specialisations that have the most potential to contribute to growth in jobs and incomes, fostering associated sectors that add value to these regional specialisations, and identifying new or emerging sectoral specialisations. The key deliverable for each region is a report that outlines the region's significant future economic opportunities and identifies the actions that would most effectively stimulate economic development and increase incomes and jobs in the region over a short- to medium-term horizon (up to 10 years).

MBIE and MPI acknowledge that achieving the economic aspirations of a region is dependent on collaboration and the ability to attract investment. Collaboration, in turn, requires inclusive processes encompassing a broad range of regional economic and social actors. However, where regional economic actors favour sectoral specialisations that are at variance with the policies of central government, there needs to be much more constructive engagement by central government than has occurred on some occasions.

For example, several regions have identified as a specialisation the global interest in food and other products that are free of genetically modified (GM) organisms. Hastings District Council became the first local authority in the country to ban GM crops and animals under its District Plan. This was strongly supported by many Hawke's Bay food producers, who had formed an organisation, Pure Hawke's Bay, to advocate for environmental regulation to ban GM organisms in crops and animals in the district.

The rule was seen as significant for economic development because of the premium attached to non-GM food by global consumers. Hastings District accounts for a large part of Hawke's Bay's food production and the council's District Plan was amended to prohibit the release and field trials of GM crops and animals. Pure Hawke's Bay drew comparisons with other high-value food-producing regions such as Burgundy, Champagne and Provence in France, and Tuscany in Italy, that had also sought to protect their GM-free status in response to consumer demand.

Hastings mayor Lawrence Yule acknowledged the argument under-pinning the District Plan rule that being able to claim GM-free status created a competitive advantage, asserting that '[w]e produce some of the best food in the world. There is a premium for GM-free food and we think that for the 10-year life of the District Plan we should use that to our advantage in terms of a market opportunity' (cited in Hendery, 2015). This was also recognised by a multi-million-dollar produce exporter, John Bostock: 'Returns for premium products are strong and growing. This added value for our producers reinforces the view that Hawke's Bay's economic prosperity lies with premium, uniquely pure and GM Free exports' (cited in Hendery, 2015).

In response to the Hastings District Council District Plan rule, and to similar provisions being considered by councils elsewhere (e.g. the Auckland, Whangarei District and Far North District councils), successive ministers for the environment have asserted that any local regulation is not feasible and that the GM regulation would be best set at a national level by the Environmental Protection Authority.

In tourism as well as food production, New Zealand's '100% Pure' brand has created significant opportunities for many regions. In some cases, regions struggle to gain a share of the economic benefits of tourism because of inadequate marketing by national tourism organisations. A recent and very stark example is Venture Taranaki's goal of promoting the Pouakai Crossing as an alternative or additional 'Great Walk' to relieve some of the pressure on the Tongariro Alpine Crossing (Wilkinson, 2016). As a result of the pressure on the main international tourist axis of Auckland–Rotorua–Queenstown–Milford Sound (which also includes the Tongariro Alpine Crossing) alternative destinations need to be marketed and tourist infrastructure enhanced.

In addition, to the extent that regional economic development associated with nature conservation is linked to domestic and international tourists, investment by central government (in particular, through funding for the Department of Conservation) will be needed to support the restoration, protection and enhancement of New Zealand's natural assets. The conservation estate makes up a third of the country, yet underfunding of the Department of Conservation has resulted in serious biodiversity decline (Brown, Stephens, Peart & Fedder, 2015). Increased funding by central agencies in the tourism, transport, technology and conservation sectors is needed to support regional innovation related to the conservation estate.

Conclusion

The discussion in this chapter, as well as that in the literature, on urban and regional entrepreneurialism highlights some vital components of success in overcoming the potential tyranny of distance associated with New Zealand's topography. These include: (1) healthy local–central government relationships in which there is mutual respect and recognition for each sphere of government's unique purpose and equitable funding arrangements; (2) effective local political leadership; (3) application of technology to industry and encouraging the attraction and retention of creative people and firms with a special emphasis on the IT sector; (4) attention to social cohesion, especially where there may be growing gaps between highly skilled, low-skilled and unskilled groups; and (5) enhancement of environmental quality. This last is important because the overall liveability and quality of the environment is an important factor in attracting and retaining skilled workers in regions.

When seeking solutions to uneven regional economic development, examples of regional innovation can be instructive and indeed empowering. However, critical success factors also need to be identified and the challenges need to be recognised. The material above cannot provide the necessary in-depth analysis that would reveal all of the potential contributors to success, or indeed provide a comprehensive assessment of the outcomes of innovation. For example, the importance of networks between local, regional and national (and even international) stakeholders, or of individual personality, have not been explored. And, very importantly, a strong regional identity — which appears to be a powerful force in the regional innovations outlined above — should not be underestimated as a driver of innovation.

Industrial restructuring is a perennial feature of modern economies internationally — as seen, for example, in de-industrialisation in the steel (rust) belt of Europe and the United States. The shift to service-sector economies, technological change and, increasingly, climate change will hasten further economic change at the regional level. With adequate research and analysis, trends can be identified and change can be planned for, not merely reacted to.

The recent growth in the literature on 'smart decline' (to complement the literature on 'smart growth') and the recognition of the need to plan for shrinkage are part of the planning and policy response (Panagopoulos & Barreira, 2012; Sousa & Pinho, 2013). Another policy response is 'right-sizing' (Hummel, 2015). These responses generally comprise proactive interventions involving relevant stakeholders, in contrast with a market-led approach. The latter has been dominant in New Zealand and has meant that many regions have been struggling with decline.

Indeed, the costs of the growth of Auckland and, looking more widely, the golden triangle of Auckland, Hamilton and Tauranga, are being borne by ratepayers in businesses and households in regions far from Auckland. This needs to change. These regions offer significant lifestyle benefits (including more affordable housing) and economic opportunities. High levels of both in-bound migration and tourism are providing some stimulus to some regions, but what is also needed is support from central government for regional innovation.

As the regional innovations discussed above indicate, there is considerable potential for the growth of tourism outside the traditional axis of Auckland, Rotorua and Queenstown, and also for technology-enhanced economic growth and innovation in all regions of New Zealand. Those of us who choose to live in New Zealand's regions know that there is considerable scope for innovation, quite apart from the growth opportunities associated with migration and tourism. The key is to have a coordinated approach. The current Regional Growth Programme is a tentative start to such an approach and needs to be expanded and independently reviewed to ensure that it achieves its goals.

Ultimately, however, developing effective local and regional interventions is best led by local government, rather than central government, as local government's purpose is, to paraphrase the earlier quote from Bush, to ensure that people in New Zealand's diverse communities with differing needs have the means to actively determine the nature and meeting of those needs. Local government cannot act on its own, and the regional innovations described above have incorporated different local stakeholders — not just other councils but often iwi and central government, too. It is the balance in any joint approach that is critical: central government must not dominate. It will be essential for those subnational agencies involved in economic and community development to work closely with iwi, whose economic importance is increasing as a result of the Treaty settlement process, even if the constitutional importance of iwi has yet to be acknowledged by many local government initiatives.

References

Brown, M. A., Stephens, R. T., Peart, R., & Fedder, B. (2015). *Vanishing nature: Facing New Zealand's biodiversity crisis*. Auckland: Environmental Defence Society.

Bush, G. (1995). *Local Government and Politics in New Zealand* (2nd ed.). Auckland: Auckland University Press.

Eaqub, S., & Stephenson, J. (2014). Regional economies. Shape, performance and drivers. NZIER public discussion paper. Working paper 2014/03. Wellington: New Zealand Institute of Economic Research. Retrieved from https://nzier.org.nz/static/media/filer_public/e4/1f/e41f5c81-2d63-4548-8859-2dad5c8e213f/nzier_public_discussion_document_2014-03-regional_economies.pdf

Hendery, S. (2015, 11 September). 'Major economic opportunity' as Hastings District Council goes GM-free. East Hastings: *Hawke's Bay Today*.

Hummel, D. (2015). Right-sizing cities in the United States: Defining its strategies. *Journal of Urban Affairs, 37(4)*, 397–409. doi:10.1111/juaf.12150

Key, J. (2016, 27 January). Key's state of the nation — full speech. Auckland: *New Zealand Herald*. Retrieved from http://www.nzherald.co.nz/nz/news/article.cfm?c_id=1&objectid=11580485 (28 January 2016).

Panagopoulos, T., & Barreira, A. P. (2012). Shrinkage perceptions and smart growth strategies for the municipalities of Portugal. Retrieved from http://ezproxy.massey.ac.nz/login?url=http://search.ebscohost.com/login.aspx?direct=true&db=edsrca&AN=rcaap.portugal.10400.1.3984&site=eds-live&scope=site

Sousa, S., & Pinho, P. (2013). Planning for shrinkage: Paradox or paradigm. *European Planning Studies, 23(1)*, 12–32. doi:10.1080/09654313.2013.820082

Statistics New Zealand. (2015). Local authority statistics. Retrieved from http://www.stats.govt.nz/browse_for_stats/government_finance/local_government/local-authority-statistics-info-releases.aspx (20 December 2015).

Venture Southland. (2015). *Year in Review 2014–15*. Invercargill: Venture Southland. Retrieved from http://www.venturesouthland.co.nz/Portals/0/Documents/Venture%20Southland%20Year%20in%20Review%202014-15.pdf

Wilkinson, J. (2016, 13 February). Long its tourism curse, Taranaki's isolation could soon be its biggest selling point. New Plymouth: *Taranaki Daily News*. Retrieved from http://www.stuff.co.nz/taranaki-daily-news/news/76493726/long-its-tourism-curse-taranakis-isolation-could-soon-be-its-biggest-selling-point (16 February 2016).

The future is young: How the regions can address youth underachievement

Dan Henderson
Mayors Taskforce for Jobs

The future is young: How the regions can address youth underachievement

Breaking down the concept of 'local economic development' requires a broad level of knowledge, networks and expertise for it to work. This is not to suggest that there needs to be a specific strategy or set of actions in order for it to occur. Instead, this term means using local people with local ideas and approaches for local outcomes. More specifically, councils in regional New Zealand are showing that being small is in fact powerful when it comes to developing local economies, and that they are best placed within their communities to influence the shape and journey of their economy.

The model is simple — for an economy to grow, it needs people. With the baby boomer generation ageing and retiring, local economies and communities now rely on young people. That said, young people demand an attractive local economy that provides opportunity and a comfortable lifestyle, so there is not a simple fix for this complex situation. Additionally, given the differing issues that communities face — such as population decline, skill shortages and growing unemployment — the prospect of a young person living their entire life in one region has become less of a reality.

Local government recognises that young people are critical to the sustainable future of communities. It emphasises not only the need to better support youth as a whole but also to assist young people to unlock their potential to positively contribute to the local economy.

In addition, the gap in the labour market between supply and demand continues to grow across all communities in New Zealand. The education sector is not equipping young people with the right skills and requirements to fill the gaps and demands of industry. As a result, the rate of young people (aged 15–24) not in employment, education or training (NEET) continues to rise, with a little over 82,000 NEETs recorded nationwide in March 2016 according to Statistics New Zealand's Household Labour Force Survey. The results of this survey also suggest that young people continue to be unemployed for longer periods of time, with around 47 per cent of all job-seekers remaining unemployed for two months or more. In addition, even when young people have been active participants in the education sector, this doesn't always translate into a career opportunity in the same field at the end of it. With all of this in mind, the future for young people, and communities, is bleak. Therefore, local councils and communities must take the lead in influencing and reversing these trends.

Councils throughout New Zealand see employment initiatives with a specific focus on young people as a key part of growing their local economy. Not only do these initiatives provide an economic benefit for the community, but they also assist these young people to counter issues that traditional social initiatives have struggled to resolve for some time.

In this chapter, we showcase a variety of councils and the approach each has taken to try to unlock the potential of its local young people. Each council and the situation it finds itself in is different; what remains consistent is the culture of small-town New Zealand and the simplicity of focusing on local connections to better assist and support young people in making a positive contribution to the local economy.

Kawerau/Matamata-Piako collaboration: Seamless boundaries

The Kawerau District is situated in the Eastern Bay of Plenty in New Zealand's principal forestry region, and represents the smallest council area by land mass in the country. Its population is small, but contains a large contingent of young people under 25 years of age and has one of the highest percentages of Māori and Pasifika people in New Zealand. Kawerau's youth population currently finds it difficult to find employment within the district, due to the maturing wood-processing industry. In addition, Māori culture attaches importance to retaining youth within the whānau, so relocation to other areas is challenging and often unsustainable for Māori youth — pressure to stay, or to return home, is common.

The Matamata-Piako District is located in the heart of the Waikato region and has some of the best-quality soils in New Zealand, making it one of the cornerstones of the country's dairy industry. The district has a large proportion of Pākehā and, like many rural areas in New Zealand, the population is ageing and this trend is being accelerated by the sustained net migration loss of young people. In an area that has a booming dairy industry, employment is always easy to find. However, this has meant that employers with unfilled job vacancies have to look to other areas of New Zealand, or overseas, for employees in order for supply to meet demand.

Despite their demographic differences and almost opposing attitudinal differences, both districts are experiencing challenges in the engagement and retention of a local entry-level workforce. A sector of Kawerau youth has low life expectations and self-confidence, whereas youth in Matamata-Piako have a well-developed sense of entitlement and expectation. These characteristics are becoming increasingly prevalent throughout New Zealand as the economic inequality gap widens.

The Seamless Boundaries project began with Matamata-Piako mayor Jan Barnes identifying that a large local employer, Silver Fern Farms, had struggled to find the available workforce to fill jobs in their two local meat-freezing works. In contrast, Kawerau mayor Malcolm Campbell knew that many young people (under 25 years old) were unemployed and seeking employment in his area but there weren't the local jobs to align them with. Both mayors understood that a 'one size fits all' approach was not appropriate or effective in this situation, and wanted to explore an innovative initiative that aimed to assist both communities by translocating a workforce from one district to the other.

Although the complexities around finding vacant jobs and an available workforce were partly solved, it was important that both communities were connected and felt a sense of ownership over this initiative. Both councils connected with key local stakeholders in the planning stages of the initiative, and opened up ongoing communication channels to make certain that it was something the community actually required.

For Kawerau specifically, a number of difficulties required attention; especially the perceived issue of exporting local young people out of the community and placing them in an area some distance away. The level of pastoral care and support required for the young people involved, their whānau and the community as a whole was not discounted, and is the critical factor in why this initiative was successful.

Another vital part of the process was the strong relationship of trust that had to be established between the employer and the two communities. Because of the complexities involved with the process and the young people themselves, each party had to be sure that what it was doing was right for whānau, each community and the employer.

In mid 2015, 33 young people from Kawerau were relocated to a local Silver Fern Farms freezing works in the Matamata-Piako District. They were provided with housing close to the factory and training opportunities to acquire all of the right skills and the NZQA qualification required to work at the factory. The initiative had a 90 per cent success rate in terms of the Kawerau young people finishing their qualification and obtaining a full-time role within Silver Fern Farms. Prior to this initiative, the success rate at the factories involved had been around 15 per cent.

Success was again put down to the pastoral support that was ongoing throughout the entire process. Silver Fern Farms commented that having someone local and connected with the young people prior to any interview or trial taking place meant that a filtering process could take place, and expectations and rules could be spoken about at an early stage. It also meant that during the young people's training, any issues could be met head-on and dealt with in a timely fashion rather than being addressed through traditional workplace disciplinary action.

The system put in place by the initiative between the two communities is now ongoing and has provided families with a steady income, which had previously been non-existent. This type of system has also been popular in other regions, as demand has only increased both for employers to find an available workforce and for young people to acquire a much-needed job and pathway.

The Seamless Boundaries project is a great example of how simple conversations and collaboration can have major benefits across communities. An idea that grew from a conversation between two rural mayors meant that not only were they able to contribute positively towards their local economies, but they were also able to influence social issues that these young people, and the community, had been facing for many years beforehand.

Clutha District: 'Handbraked' economies

The Clutha District is a rural area in South Otago. It has a population of around 16,500 and is spread out over nine small communities, Balclutha being the largest. The district is unique in that although it is small in terms of population, it has a number of businesses that employ a large number of people. Because of this, there tend to be plenty of local opportunities available, but it has not always been easy to align local people with these opportunities. Consequently, there has been a 'handbrake' applied to the economy.

When Bryan Cadogan won the mayoral election in 2010, he soon found that he had a crisis to attend to. It was clear what needed to be achieved; the question was how to articulate this in a plan that employers and young people would buy into, and which would also be sustainable for the community beyond his time as mayor.

The first major task in the journey was to engage with the employers in the district and seek their view on what issues they were currently facing, as well as highlighting where things were working well and where there might be opportunities for the Clutha District. One issue quickly became apparent: the district was awash with job vacancies. Hundreds of jobs were not being filled and were making employers start to think about relocating into bigger areas with a larger pool of potential employees. The situation was made more difficult by the population of the district being in continuous decline over the past 20 years. It was clear that it was now or never for the local council and community to take action.

The issue was confronting for the local community; only 30 years previously the area had suffered from underemployment and from the compromises that had to be made, both on an individual and on a community level, just to get by, yet now it was facing the 'crisis' of a surplus of jobs for which employers couldn't find the available workforce quickly enough.

Effectively addressing this issue had the potential to fundamentally change the trajectory of the district's rural communities, halting the decline in population and the withdrawal of services. It seemed a reasonably simple equation — if the community could fill some of the estimated 700 jobs on offer, things could turn themselves around, not only economically but also for the people, especially youth. And so began a number of initiatives designed to let the 'handbrake' off.

First, there was the Ready Steady Work programme that runs for five weeks every year with the aim of gathering up all the local unemployed youth and learning more about them and their interests, while also utilising the position of the mayor to gather together the major employers in the area to be part of the process. The low-impact and informal-style job interviews involved remove any barriers, simply putting a person that wants a job in front of a person that wants an employee. This started a process that flowed very easily into a successful outcome for all parties.

The next initiative came about through adversity — when the district was hit with the worst round of redundancies in its history, with three of the largest sawmills being placed in receivership and closed within only a few months. The initiative took the concept of speed-dating and morphed it into an innovative way of doing job interviews. The concept was simple: gather the employers in a room together with the redundant workforce, sit them across a table from each other — two people, two minutes, too easy. Once again it worked, showing that the fastest way to move the district forward was to not allow it to move backwards.

The next evolution occurred when it became obvious that job numbers were too large to be filled internally within the district. At one point, local youth unemployment numbers dropped to just two people; so it became time to search further afield (while still continuing to fill job vacancies locally).

This time the initiative took the form of a job festival. Local employers agreed to travel to the nearest city (Dunedin), advertise their job situations to the university, polytechnic and job-seekers generally, and take part in another 'speed-dating for jobs' exercise to fill the available jobs they had.

Again, it was a success. Some of the Dunedinites who acquired jobs through this event commuted to their new jobs, returning home each day to inject money into their local economy, while others shifted to Clutha. Either way, both contributed to the Clutha economy by providing the much-needed additional workforce that these employers had been demanding for some time.

The Clutha District is now into its fifth year of collaboration with local employers, and initiatives are starting to become more structured and sustainable, primarily through the district council's Long Term Plan. This work has indirectly been linked to the initiation of a new 65-section residential subdivision in Balclutha because of the high demand for accommodation for workers; initial investigations are also under way for a similar development in another local town, Milton, where demand is also high. The community is now looking into the development of a major industrial park in Balclutha and the positive momentum is spreading, with many locals coming up with their own plans to be a part of this development.

Throughout the district, people are increasingly seeing the potential to move Clutha forward; and it began with an emphasis on the younger generation.

Manawatū/Palmerston North collaboration: Talent Central

The concept of Talent Central arose in the minds of those in the Manawatū District and Palmerston North City who were concerned that these areas needed a sustainable workforce to underpin the agribusiness strategy that the region had embarked on four years previously. Situated in the heart of the North Island, the area is one of the hubs for innovation, especially in the agricultural sector, so it was important that both communities addressed the issues surrounding their workforces. Once a local regional growth strategy for the eight local government councils in the Manawatū region had been created, it became necessary to navigate the terrain between education and employment, where the lines had so often been blurred.

In simple terms, there was a major local disconnect between the skills of those leaving the education system (supply) and the skills required for local jobs by the business community (demand). The Manawatū District and Palmerston North City wanted to attract and retain the 'talent' in their region, and identify the key influencers that had to be addressed in order to do this.

In the same way that the agribusiness strategy came about, the two councils began with a conversation. A steering group was formed, comprising those most acutely aware of the disconnect between education and employment. It was initially named Manawatū Youth Futures. The aim from the beginning was to provide a line of sight through meaningful pathways that would enable young people to make informed choices about their futures. As the conversation progressed, it became apparent that if the school principals weren't supportive and willing to open their doors to businesspeople, then the overall aim would be jeopardised.

Confidence in the vision grew with many large local businesses and industries pledging their support, but again the principals needed to see the wisdom in collaborating with the business community. An interesting exercise involved shifting schools' thinking from a deficit model focused on young people disengaging from education and being unemployable, to realising that focusing on the 95 per cent who were actively engaged would make more sense.

The Manawatū is the agribusiness capital of New Zealand, but it is not all about growing grass. The key to maintaining and enhancing success is growing great people, being innovative and ensuring that the region can attract and retain people with the necessary skills. Talent Central became the new name of the framework, to reflect the underlying objectives and themes of the region.

Talent Central is based on three pillars that extend and grow the Manawatū's leadership, foster innovation at all ages and in all types of employment, and create pathways for students from education to employment. The approach of Talent Central is all-encompassing, involving everyone from early childhood, through primary school and secondary school to tertiary study and employment.

Regional growth occurs when talent and industry in a region combine, and it relies on a balance between the skills being generated and the skills needed by industry. The reality is that there is a mismatch between these skills; a gap between matching the talent in the region with the opportunities available right now. A framework was clearly needed to better connect people with ideas and possibilities that would help shape the future of the region. Talent Central is community, education and industry all working together to create sustainable futures for the talent in a region. It will operate as a brokerage hub where people looking for talent to make things happen are matched with those who want to make a contribution.

Through building this thorough and robust framework, the region has secured the support of all of the region's secondary schools, who will contribute seed funding to kick the framework off, as have local tertiary providers Massey University and the Universal College of Learning (UCOL). As a result of this support, a trust was formed that includes representation from the local Chamber of Commerce, the Youth Guarantees Network (Ministry of Education), the Youth Engineers Scheme and the Mayors Taskforce for Jobs.

Early success has seen the scholarships programme take off, with the first raft of scholarships focusing on the agribusiness sector being given out to students in Years 9–11. Each scholarship is worth $500 and the students are selected from each of the schools involved. They are responsible for promoting their experience with their fellow students and in some cases engaging them in a project sponsored by business. The aim of this specific work stream is to have 25 students per year engaging in a programme that will allow them to see the full spectrum of primary-sector careers. It is designed to inspire and motivate students about a career in the agribusiness sector, whether that is on the farm, in a lab or in a boardroom.

The work streams that Talent Central rolls out will all look to give young people the opportunity to learn what it is like working within different sectors, which will help them understand and better clarify their own interests, learn about their own strengths and weaknesses, and explore the various pathways and opportunities that are available within the region. Talent Central will be further developed over time, looking to be transitioned into the new local economic development agency, the Central Economic Development Agency (CEDA), and to include a business hub in Palmerston North City and a satellite hub in Feilding.

This Talent Central idea is a great example of how two councils have collaborated, not only with each other but also with their entire community, to bring about system change. It was important that there was a change in approach, and a change in system, as the status quo of ad hoc programmes working towards different aims was neither sustainable nor beneficial for the community. The Talent Central concept is a centralised, multi-sector approach that has the best interests of the community at heart, which is why it has gained so much momentum so quickly.

Conclusion

As has been illustrated in this chapter, for councils in New Zealand there is little benefit in relying on the ageing workforce to fill the fast-approaching jobs vacuum — the emphasis must be on young people!

Young people not only have a lifetime of productivity ahead of them, but they also offer a new approach to life and are best placed to manage the ever-changing world of technology and innovation.

Unlocking the potential of young people is a phrase that rolls off the tongue quite easily; however, operationalising this notion certainly isn't as straightforward. It takes a great deal of engagement, consultation, research and, most importantly, patience to understand the critical factors of doing this at a community level.

Although statistics may give a negative impression, they do exemplify the amount of opportunity that is being lost and the room there is for communities to grow, both physically and economically. These statistics suggest that young people have become less employable and less productive, and are therefore of less value to the economy. Local government completely disagrees.

There simply needs to be a shift in focus to address the main concerns: the growing gap between education and employment, and why this picture continues to worsen. The mismatch between supply and demand does not need to be complicated; what's important is making a concerted effort to support young people, and ensuring that local opportunities can be aligned with local young people.

As can be seen from each of the three cases presented, while these councils all have different environments and challenges they are all able to connect with community at a pace and manner that most others cannot. These examples show that mayors, councils and communities are committed to influencing and bettering not only the local economy but also, more importantly, the lives of the people who live in and contribute to that economy. Moreover, local government has had to evolve its own thinking to incorporate not only local industry being a key to the economy but also how it can better influence the process to 'feed' local industry more effectively.

Local economies, especially those in regional locations in New Zealand, need to be attractive. They need local people solving local issues. Most importantly, however, they need a sustainable future. Never has there been a more important time for local governments to be at the centre of shaping their local economy and determining how it should grow in the future. So why go anywhere else when local governments have the answers? After all, they are the elected representatives voted in by community, for community.

7. The peculiar case of Canterbury

Lana Hart
Workplace diversity advisor, Christchurch
Carl Davidson
Research First, Christchurch

The peculiar case of Canterbury

Canterbury's story of economic transformation begins with a natural disaster, but is driven by the inflow of migrants. As a consequence, not only is the region's economy transformed, but its cultural life will never be the same.

Canterbury's economy, like that of the rest of the country, was beginning to show signs of recovery from the global financial crisis (GFC). New Zealand's economy experienced five quarters of negative economic growth between March 2008 and March 2009, but then started to grow — albeit slowly — through 2010. Canterbury entered into recession later than the rest of the country, thanks to strong commodity prices, and was also growing faster than the country as a whole in 2010.

The local economic development agency, the Canterbury Development Corporation (CDC), had an economic development strategy in place that covered the years 2009 to 2014 and envisioned a region where 'Canterbury is a world leading economy founded on innovation, diversity, and sustainability: a region that is a great place to live, learn, work, visit, invest, and do business for all' (as stated by the CDC in 2009). Within this plan for the region, the CDC was looking to position Christchurch as the hub of the South Island, working as a counterweight to the development of the Auckland economy.

An important part of this plan was building on the quality of life in the region, and using this to attract 'smart' people, capital and businesses. Interestingly, the CDC noted that at that time Canterbury's population was less diverse than the national average, suggesting that the region had been less successful in attracting migrants than other parts of New Zealand.

Before the CDC's vision could be realised, at 4.35 a.m. on 4 September

2010 a magnitude 7.1 earthquake hit the city.[1] For a number of technical reasons (mixed with a good measure of luck), there were no fatalities. However, this earthquake — and its many aftershocks — did substantial damage to the buildings and infrastructure of the city's central business district (CBD).[2] A state of emergency was declared for the city, and the CBD was closed to the general public. Economic activity in the city was significantly reduced, and business confidence declined sharply. These were all serious blows to the region's economy; but it was also clear that rebuilding would drive increased economic activity. Indeed, estimates at this time suggested that upwards of NZ$5 billion would be spent on repairing and rebuilding the city.

But then, at 12.51 p.m. on 22 February 2011, another major earthquake hit the city. This 6.3-magnitude earthquake was centred closer to Christchurch and was also shallower,[3] and it hit the city during the lunch hour on a workday. As a result it was much more destructive than the September 2010 event and far more deadly. The earthquake caused widespread damage, killed 185 people and injured thousands. Christchurch's central city and its eastern suburbs were hit particularly hard, and the in-ground (horizontal) infrastructure was damaged throughout the city. The Central City Red Zone was established on the day of the earthquake as an exclusion zone in the CBD. Central Christchurch, it

---

1   The earthquake was centred 40 kilometres west of Christchurch, close to the settlement of Darfield.

2   There was also significant damage done to the township of Kaiapoi, north of Christchurch.

3   The authors, like almost everyone currently living in Christchurch, now know far more about the arcane art of measuring the intensity of earthquakes. As well as understanding the competing scales for measuring the size of earthquakes, one needs to distinguish between an earthquake's epicentre and its hypocentre.

seemed, would not be accessible by residents for many months and, in some parts, years.

The Canterbury Earthquake Recovery Agency (CERA) was established in response to the February earthquake to lead and coordinate the ongoing recovery effort. The agency was given wide-ranging powers, including the ability to suspend laws and regulations for the purpose of earthquake recovery. CERA's purpose was 'to lead and partner with communities to return greater Christchurch to a prosperous and thriving place to work, live and play, as quickly as possible'. The task facing CERA, and everyone in Christchurch, was immense: 70 per cent of the buildings in the CBD had been destroyed, and across the city over 175,000 buildings were damaged and in need of repair. More than 10,000 buildings needed to be demolished, and over 17,000 new houses needed to be built. The horizontal infrastructure was severely damaged ('seriously munted', in the unforgettable words of the mayor at the time, Bob Parker). Prime Minister John Key summed up the damage best when he said, 'This is not the Christchurch we knew; it's closer to a war zone.'

Given the scale of the damage, the estimates of the repair costs were colossal. Rebuilding the 'munted' horizontal infrastructure alone was costed at NZ$2 billion. Treasury's initial estimates of the total bill were NZ$20 billion (10% of GDP), but by April 2013 these estimates had grown to NZ$40 billion. In 2016, the CDC estimated that the rebuild had added at least 10 per cent to Christchurch's traditional underlying economy. To put that into perspective, this means that the rebuild programme is worth as much to Christchurch as its accommodation, hospitality and retail sectors combined. Financial services firm JPMorgan Chase & Co says that the total overall losses related to this earthquake may be as much as US$12 billion — which would make it the third most costly earthquake event in history, after the 2011 Japan and 1994 California earthquakes. These costs would be met by a mix of private insurance (and their reinsurers overseas) and the state through agencies such as the government-owned Earthquake Commission (EQC).[4]

The Minister for Canterbury Earthquake Recovery Gerry Brownlee established a special unit within CERA, called the Christchurch Central Development Unit (CCDU), to create a recovery plan for the central city. Over a remarkable 100 days, the CCDU pulled together what is known as The Blueprint, which offers a framework for the redevelopment of the city.

The Blueprint outlines the form for rebuilding the city and defines what are known as the anchor projects (such as the Metro Sports facility and the Christchurch Bus Exchange) to stimulate development of the city.

With both a plan in place for the recovery of Christchurch and funding to deliver it, the real challenge facing the city following the earthquakes was the supply of labour. A labour demand model developed by the CDC[5] predicted that the city would need an extra 37,000 workers by the height of the rebuild. The key word here is 'extra': this prediction was for the labour demand *in addition to* fully mobilising the local supply of labour.

Space prevents a full discussion of the many initiatives that emerged to support (and sometimes to oppose) CERA's recovery blueprint. Private developers, largely local, reinvested quickly and brought new and exciting premises to market; initiatives like ReStart, EPIC and Gap Filler all made (and continue to make) important contributions to the recovery of the city.

---

4   It is important to note that a significant local insurer, AMI, was supported by the Crown to the value of NZ$500 million. This led to the sale of AMI to AIG.

5   Along with the consultancy Market Economics and the Department of Labour (now subsumed into the Ministry of Business, Innovation and Employment).

Among a range of initiatives, the Crown established the Canterbury Employ-ment and Skills Board (CESB) in late 2011 to determine the state of the labour market in Christchurch following the earthquakes and to plan for the skills and workforce needs. CESB's mission was to 'ensure that skills and talents needs do not become an impediment to the rebuilding of Canterbury'.

In many ways, the CESB was established to respond to concerns that the labour market would not be able to adjust quickly enough to meet the additional demand presented by the rebuild. The Crown was also cognisant that it was important that the rapid expansion of demand for talent and skills in Christchurch did not impact on labour markets in other parts of New Zealand.

Speaking at a conference for industry training organisations in 2011, Alex Bouma, the deputy chair of CESB at the time, described the challenge of meeting the rebuild's skills and talent needs as being the industry training sector's 'moonshot'. Bouma referenced John F. Kennedy's famous 1963 Rice University speech in which he asserted, 'we choose to go to the Moon not because it is easy but because it is hard, because that goal will serve to organize and measure the best of our energies and skills'.

To help 'organise and measure' the skills and talent needs, the CESB recommended four strategic initiatives. These were:

1. enabling smoother (and quicker) transitions into the labour market
2. connecting business with education and training
3. enhancing labour productivity
4. attracting and retaining skilled staff to the city.

While not always in concert, central government, local government and the private sector began working in a number of ways to address all four of these initiatives. One notable example was Collaborate Canterbury which, from 2011, matched local construction businesses with businesses outside the region (both internationally and domestically) to source labour and other resources. Two years following its establishment by the Canterbury Employers' Chamber of Commerce ('The Chamber'), it received funding from central government.

The need to look outside the region for the necessary skills and talent was obvious, and pressing. The scale and range of the skills needed for the rebuild were staggering: geotechnical engineers, quantity surveyors, building consent officers, project managers and experienced carpenters were all in high demand. At the same time, there was also high demand for labourers and semi-skilled workers.

Responding to these demands required fresh thinking by local employers. Offshore recruitment was new to many businesses, and job fairs in England and Australia offered straightforward ways for businesses to engage with job-seekers in comparable labour markets. Local recruitment agencies with international experience grew increasingly busy, and those with links to the vast export workforce of the Philippines enjoyed an advantage in the suddenly scaled-up labour market. Larger construction companies, especially those whose individual staff had experience in large overseas projects, soon capitalised on this knowledge by running overseas recruitment drives themselves.

As a result of efforts such as these (and the international publicity the earthquakes generated), migration to Christchurch burgeoned. In the 2006 Census, 82 per cent of Cantabrians were born in New Zealand compared with a national average of 77 per cent. Of those born overseas, the vast majority were born in Great Britain. The number of work visas granted in Canterbury ran at about a quarter of Auckland's. By 2013–14 and with the Canterbury rebuild well under way, these work visa figures were over 60 per cent of Auckland numbers. The sharp rise in work visas was accompanied by a decline in student and permanent resident visa applications.[6]

Filipino workers formed the largest part of the temporary workforce. The Philippines had already become the leading source country for work visas in Canterbury back in 2007–08. Migrant workers were arriving in large numbers to work on the increasing number of dairy farm conversions across Canterbury (with dairying becoming an industry increasingly reliant on migrant labour). Following the earthquakes, the number of migrant workers from the Philippines mushroomed. By 2015–16, Filipino work visa figures outstripped British work visas by more than two to one. Of around the 32,000 work visas approved for work in Canterbury since 2010,[7] over 9200 were approved for Filipinos while only 4490 were approved for British migrants.

The inflow of migrants to Christchurch meant that the city became visibly more multicultural. Before the earthquakes, Christchurch had sometimes been described as 'the most English of New Zealand's cities', but this is no longer the case. Irish, Indian and Filipino residents are seen and heard throughout the region, from Ashburton's schools and Selwyn's basketball courts to Christchurch's pub scene and newly revived Catholic churches. A major construction company built a Filipino workers' camp near the small town of Oxford in North Canterbury. On Sundays, the camp's 90 residents transformed the town into a Little Manila.

---

6   This provides an insight into the changes occurring in Christchurch during the immediate post-earthquake period. International student numbers declined (as did international tourist numbers), but the numbers of international workers reached unprecedented levels. The city became less of a destination and more of a work camp.

7   A new work visa is issued each time an applicant renews their visa. These figures therefore do not represent the number of individuals with a work visa, as they include renewals as well as first-time visas.

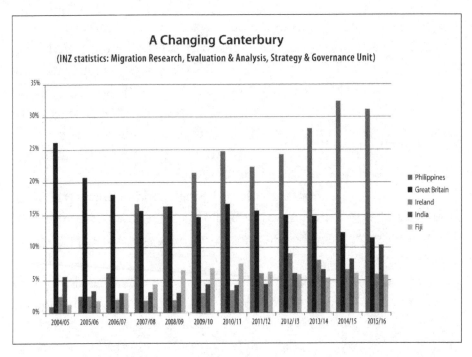

Figure 1: **Work visas approved for Canterbury, by source country as a percentage of total work visas, principal applicants only, 2004/05 to 2015/16 (Immigration New Zealand statistics)**

With so much housing stock having been damaged in the earthquakes, the city experienced a period of housing shortage. This was exacerbated by the inflow of labour to help with the rebuild, and the shortage affected the migrant communities particularly strongly. Devoid of local tenancy references or know-how, many newcomers found it difficult to secure affordable, warm and semi-permanent accommodation. Few businesses recruiting from overseas failed to consider this in their settlement support of new staff: sourcing or at least assisting with accommodation when people first arrived became nearly mandatory for companies employing new arrivals to the region. Billeting, employer-provided shared accommodation, medium-term hotel stays, renting with co-workers, and converting aged-care facilities or motels into workers' accommodation became common answers to the housing shortage in the years following the earthquakes.

Canterbury's health-care system was also affected by the rapid change in population mix. Although most holders of work visas were eligible for subsidised care under the public health-care scheme,[8] a lack of familiarity with the system and the cost of co-payments to general practitioner (GP) clinics meant that some migrants used Christchurch Hospital's emergency department as their primary health provider (thereby 'clogging up' emergency services).[9]

The media reported an increase in the incidence of sexually transmitted diseases among the new migrant population,[10] and sex workers complained that foreign clients were insisting on unsafe sexual practices. Some newcomers to Christchurch complained that GP clinics had closed their books and were no longer taking on new patients, a situation that some believed was due to the sharp increase in population.

CERA recognised that the growth in the number of migrants had created new challenges for the recovery and attempted to grapple with these through research, analysis and engagement. However, as with much in the post-earthquake environment, this experience was unprecedented and CERA was largely operating without a map. As a result, a coordinated government response to emerging population issues never eventuated. With hindsight, it is easy to see that this lack of response was due to the

---

8   Holders of work visas are entitled to enrol for publicly funded health care if their work visa is valid for two years or longer.

9   http://www.stuff.co.nz/the-press/news/9460433/Migrants-clogging-hospital

10   http://www.stuff.co.nz/national/health/9274685/Luck-of-the-Irish-has-sex-disease-downside

new and sometimes unclear role of CERA, to a range of different staff with various responsibilities in these areas, and to the heterogeneity of the new migrant population. In other words, developing a government response to the needs of Canadian building inspectors was not the same as creating a strategy to assist Sri Lankan brick-layers. Nevertheless, an opportunity was missed for CERA to demonstrate leadership in a space where leadership was required. This provides a clear lesson should other regions find themselves facing similar challenges to Christchurch.

Local and regional government had their own responses to the changing face of Canterbury. Christchurch City Council developed guidelines for engaging with migrant communities following a natural disaster, conducted a stocktake of council activities that supported new migrants to the city, and later, in response to a call from local service providers to provide leadership and focus, set about developing Christchurch's multicultural strategy.

Similarly, non-governmental organisations actively moved in to support migrant communities. The Red Cross supported a number of initiatives to support CALD (culturally and linguistically diverse) community service providers to deliver community-led recovery initiatives that would connect people, build resilience, provide psychosocial support and promote well-being for earthquake-affected CALD communities. The Christchurch Migrant Hub ran the Socially Isolated Migrant Women's Programme and funded two support workers whose focus was on connecting people into familiar community networks for faith-based institutions/sports/food outlets/medical services/remittance services, which in turn led to the building of capacity, capability and resilience.

Meanwhile, Selwyn District had become the 'fastest-growing district in New Zealand' with the previously sleepy townships of Lincoln and Rolleston now swelling with British, South African and Scottish migrants. The 11 district mayors of Canterbury gathered under the umbrella of

Environment Canterbury's Mayoral Forum to develop a regional strategy to maximise the economic growth of Canterbury following the peak of the rebuild, identifying migrant settlement as one of its seven priority work streams.

Policy interventions were adapted to the unusual features of the Canterbury labour market. In response to media coverage and research into perceived exploitation in Canterbury, and to central government's ongoing need to demonstrate that local skills would be used before there was recruitment internationally, the government initiated several changes to immigration and recruitment policies that tightened the migration requirements for those hired offshore. These changes included a new requirement for employers to engage with the Canterbury Skills and Employment Hub, a regional immigration policy designed for the situation of the Canterbury labour market, and a new agreement between the Philippines and New Zealand about fees and support for inbound Filipino workers.

These policy controls had the effect of pruning out many poor (and sometimes unethical) practices that had been reported by some in the years immediately following the earthquakes — such as migrants having paid tens of thousands of dollars to land a job in Christchurch, or informal and inexperienced recruiters operating in the Canterbury market — but also added to the processing challenges and the time that businesses had to invest into recruiting from offshore. Furthermore, the turning of the bureaucratic wheels was too slow for the demands of the labour market. It wasn't until mid 2015 that immigration rules allowed lower-skilled workers that were crucial to large-scale projects to extend their work visas to three years; at the same time, an accreditation scheme for labour hire agencies operating in the rebuild was introduced.

With the inflow of migrant workers (and the return of international tourists as the city's recovery began in earnest), the city began to change, too. New ethnic restaurants opened in and around the CBD, pubs started catering directly to Irish and British clientele, and international money transfer services were ramped up for the thousands of migrants that were sending remittances home. National banks that had seen little need for Christchurch-based migrant banking services found, post-earthquake, new resources to deliver tailored services to their new migrant customers. Some financial institutions developed entire migrant engagement strategies, involving assisting with the opening of bank accounts in people's first days in the country, hosting newcomer social and Christmas events, and delivering free financial planning advice in the migrants' workplaces.

Canterbury employers quickly learnt that hiring staff offshore required a different approach than hiring locally. New practices and resources had to be established for each business and its existing workforce to adapt to the needs of the new migrant workforce. In an unusual labour market where construction, engineering and trades skills were in high demand, businesses needed to respond to the settlement needs of their new migrant staff, such as assisting with or providing English language tuition; linking family members to information about schools, jobs, recreational activities or taxes; and providing slower, more detailed induction and training programmes to introduce the workers to the peculiarities of New Zealand workplaces. To support these changes, the government funded a programme within The Chamber to provide free support to businesses employing migrants.

Together, the new initiatives and the visible contribution that migrants were making to the rebuild of the region helped to minimise the public pushback that might have been evident if migration had suddenly increased due to other drivers. Indeed, as (previously) the most ethnically homogeneous main centre in New Zealand and a region with a reputation of provincialism and occasional xenophobia, Canterbury residents might have conformed to national perceptions and formed negative views about the new migrant population. Instead, with international workers repairing residents' homes, laying high-speed broadband on their streets, handling their EQC claims and inspecting the safety of their children's schools, it was hard not to appreciate the profound input that these newcomers were making to the city and, therefore, the locals put out the welcome mat instead of shutting doors.

To enlist the involvement of everyday Cantabrians in welcoming the region's newest residents, The Chamber led a campaign targeting not just employers and co-workers, but others in the host communities — neighbours, people sharing schools and sports clubs, local shopkeepers — who also have a role in helping to settle the international workforce. Their Start with a Smile campaign nudges people towards more meaningful and more frequent interactions between Kiwi-born and foreign-born residents.

Migrants themselves reported mostly positive social experiences. For migrants from Europe, the United Kingdom, South Africa and North America, the outdoor and adventure lifestyle was new and accessible. For those from more hierarchical cultures, such as the Philippines and India, the egalitarian Kiwi culture was an exciting, though sometimes daunting, change. Some holders of working holiday visas who were expecting a bigger party scene as part of their one- to two-year working stints sometimes complained of a quiet Christchurch with no vivid nightlife or arts scene, although others enjoyed the focus on sports and recreation.

Today, nearly all of the major construction and trades companies in Canterbury have a workforce that contains significant proportions of workers born overseas, and many small and medium businesses do too. Labour hire agencies have become key players and are now some of the largest employers of migrants in the region. Innovative retention schemes have emerged that are designed to keep skilled migrants attached to the company that made the investment to recruit them from offshore, even in a more fluid labour market where migrants can more easily change the terms of their work visas.

As we write this in 2016, Christchurch has passed the halfway point for the rebuild (in terms of dollars spent). CERA was disestablished on 18 April 2016, with a number of its functions being transferred both to existing organisations (such as the Christchurch City Council, the Canterbury District Health Board and the Ministry of Business, Innovation and Employment [MBIE]) and a number of newly created ones (such as Ōtākaro Limited and Regenerate Christchurch). Stronger Christchurch Infrastructure Rebuild Team's work on the horizontal infrastructure is entering its last phase, and the central city precinct in CERA's blueprint will soon be open.

However, it is important to note the retreat from the rebuilding peak will be a slow one (think 'plateau' rather than 'descent'). Estimates are that NZ$100 million a week is currently being spent on the rebuild and that this level of activity will continue for years to come. As a result, MBIE has noted that local labour supply is tight and will remain so for the next three years. This means that the region will continue to rely on migrant labour for the foreseeable future.

The response to the Christchurch earthquakes demonstrates how quickly central government, local government and employers can adapt. Six years ago, it was a rare Canterbury business that made fresh and effective efforts to support migrant staff throughout the extent of their settlement journeys. Today, Canterbury's workplaces have changed drastically in how they think about skills and talent, how they support their staff, and how they respond to more multicultural workplaces.

There is no doubt that the people who brought their skills to Canterbury in the aftermath of the earthquakes have been a core part of the Canterbury rebuild engine, or that a majority of the businesses that brought them here are now well-oiled cogs in the migration wheel. What is also clear is that Christchurch as a city is a more interesting place for having an unprecedented number of migrant residents. While Christchurch has better engaged with the wider world in order to recover, the real question now is: How does Christchurch draw on this engagement not just to recover but also to flourish?

8. Income inequality in New Zealand regions

**Omoniyi Alimi, David C. Maré
and Jacques Poot**
University of Waikato, and Motu
Economic and Public Policy Research

Income inequality in New Zealand regions[1]

In the eyes of the rest of the world Aotearoa New Zealand is a strikingly beautiful country with safe cities and friendly people who have a high level of prosperity that is shared fairly. This image was first shaped more than a century ago when the country led the way globally with progressive policies such as giving women the vote in 1893 and introducing minimum wages in 1894. Nowadays, tourists visiting the country's top attractions on organised tours and businesspeople staying in the comfort of Auckland's and Wellington's four-star hotels will find this perception mostly confirmed, or at least find any signs of poverty and inequality less pervasive than at home. But those who venture off the beaten tracks of metropolitan centres and main tourist destinations see a different New Zealand. Yes, the scenic

---

1   This study has been supported by the 2012–2014 *Nga Tangata Oho Mairangi* (NTOM) project, funded by Ministry of Business, Innovation and Employment (MBIE) grant CONT-29661-HASTR-MAU and the 2014–2020 *Capturing the Diversity Dividend of Aotearoa New Zealand* (CaDDANZ) project, funded by MBIE grant UOWX1404. Access to the data used in this study was provided by Statistics New Zealand under conditions designed to give effect to the security and confidentiality provisions of the Statistics Act 1975. All frequency counts using Census data were subject to base three rounding in accordance with Statistics New Zealand's release policy for census data. The views, opinions, findings and conclusions or recommendations expressed in this chapter are strictly those of the authors and do not necessarily represent, and should not be reported as, those of Statistics New Zealand or the organisations at which the authors are employed.

beauty and the friendliness of the people are ubiquitous and enduring, but prosperity may be hard to detect when travelling through depopulated towns with dilapidated storefronts and dwellings.

This sharp contrast between the glitzy CBDs and peeling paint of small-town buildings has of course not gone unnoticed in analyses of regional trends in recent years. It is indeed one of the triggers of this book. Eaqub (2014) compares median household income in New Zealand regions with GDP per capita of countries. That puts Auckland and Wellington firmly in the Western Europe league, but leaves regions such as Hawke's Bay, Gisborne and Manawatu–Wanganui more on a par with Greece, and Northland with Timor Leste. This last may appear somewhat far-fetched; but few would argue that the big city–hinterland gap has not widened in New Zealand, as it has in many developed countries. Of course, there have always been big differences between income and prosperity across geographical space, sufficiently so to generate a separate field of economics to explain the causes of such differences. And the explanation has always been, and remains, complex and debatable. Consequently, regional and urban economics was a rather unloved field of the economics profession for much of the last century, at least until the 1990s, when mainstream economists developed some new tools that enabled more rigorous explanations (see for example Krugman, 1998).

Depending on the geographical scale applied, spatial differences may have increased more in New Zealand than in many other countries, given New Zealand's long history of uniform prices and national wage determination until the reform years of the 1980s. Williamson (1965) compared regional income inequality across a range of countries and found that in the 1950s Australia and New Zealand had the lowest regional inequality of the 24 countries examined. But we have to be careful not to glamorise that 'golden age' of New Zealand's egalitarian economy, protected behind high walls of import tariffs and quotas. Jensen (1969)

Figure 1: **Average personal income for males in New Zealand regions, 2013**

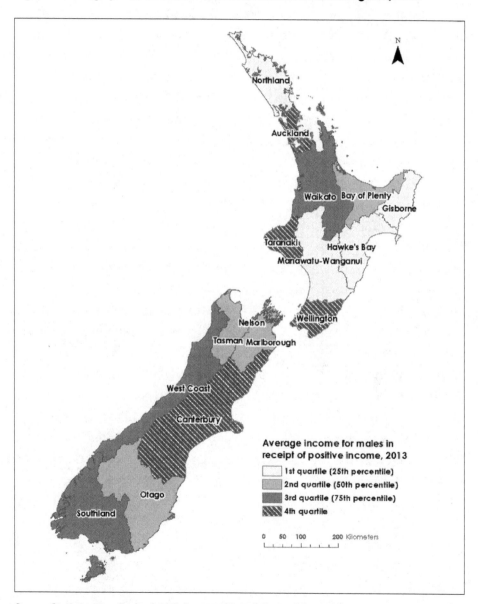

Source: Statistics New Zealand, 2013 Census of Population and Dwellings

calculated that in fiscal year 1964/65 gross personal income in the city with the highest income per capita (Invercargill at that time, with Wellington in second and Auckland in third place) was 37 per cent higher than in the poorest city (Greymouth). Compare that with 2014 regional data and Johnson (2015: 48) finds that the median personal income of those employed is 29 per cent higher in the highest-ranking region (Wellington) compared with the lowest (Manawatū-Whanganui). Eaqub (2014: 12) finds a much greater gap of 63 per cent in 2013 median household income between the highest (Auckland) and lowest (Northland) regional scores. Figure 1 shows how average personal income (as defined below) varied across New Zealand regions in 2013.

Such calculations show that there has always been a notable gap in income per capita between the richest and poorest regions of New Zealand, even if it was historically less so than in other developed countries. Additionally, due to higher average rents and house prices in metropolitan centres, the cost of living is much greater in such cities than in the provinces, so that the spatial gap in *real* average income between high-income cities and low-income hinterland is actually much less than it is in nominal terms. Indeed, real income differences between regions may be declining today, when house prices in high-income cities such as Auckland and Wellington are increasing faster than elsewhere. This observed decline is consistent with the prediction from economic theory that real income per capita differences between large regions should over time become smaller, provided that such regions, first, have access to the same technologies; second, are linked through trade; and, third, have unrestricted flows of capital and labour (see for example Le Gallo and Fingleton, 2014 for a review of the international evidence).

Accurately accounting for the way in which regional differences in prices partially or fully offset the observed gaps in nominal income between regions is quite complicated and will not be attempted in the present chapter. Statistics New Zealand does not calculate regional–spatial price indexes because it concluded, based on a lack of submissions received after seeking public consultation, that there appears to be little interest in knowing whether a dollar of income buys you more in one region than another (Statistics New Zealand, 2014: 12). We disagree with this assessment and plan to report regional–spatial price indexes in another publication. Incorporating regional differences in prices would, however, not weaken the main conclusion of this chapter, which is that there have been within all regions sharp increases in income inequality among individuals between 1986 and 2013, with the exception of the 2001–2006 phase of rapid economic growth. Additionally, differences between the average or median nominal incomes observed across regions are already small compared with the differences in income between those receiving the highest and the lowest incomes within each region. In simple terms, an individual's personal characteristics, such as education and experience, play a much bigger role in predicting personal real income than their location, although the latter is by no means irrelevant.

The issue, therefore, is not primarily one of growing differences in average income between regions, but one of increasing inequality within regions and the ways in which this growing intra-regional inequality manifests itself differently in different places. The latter is aptly shown by Johnson (2015), who concludes that the main underlying driver of unequal opportunities across individuals is that of agglomeration: the concentration of people and capital in modern, globally connected, knowledge-intensive and services-driven cities versus the relative population decline of the provinces. This process, lucidly explained in Glaeser's (2011) *The Triumph of the City*, implies that spatial differences in average income are becoming less meaningful for understanding the changes in economic fortunes of individuals who have increasingly diverse backgrounds and face a growing diversity of circumstances.

In this chapter we therefore focus predominantly on how income inequality within each of the regions has increased. We do this by updating, by means of post-millennium data, Karagedikli et al.'s (2000) analysis of income inequality between and within New Zealand's 16 regions. In the next section we show how each region has fared in terms of average personal income relative to the nation. This is followed by a discussion, by means of several measures, of how regions have differed in terms of changes in their distribution of personal incomes. In the final section we draw some broad conclusions and reinforce our main point: that comparing the average income of regions is less helpful for understanding the mixed fortunes that individuals in different regions (and different parts of regions) face than understanding their widely varying backgrounds and the circumstances they face. Indeed, growing intra-regional inequality is a big issue all regions have experienced, albeit not uniformly. Despite the decline in the real cost of communication and transportation, location and distance paradoxically matter more now for opportunities of some population sub-groups than in the past, particularly those with lower skills and at older ages. As such, growing intra-regional income inequality is unlikely to be effectively addressed with 'space-blind' policies. Recent policies 'nudging' migrant settlement and new investment in non-metropolitan areas in order to boost demand there appear consistent with that perspective.

Average personal income: differences between New Zealand regions

As noted above, New Zealand income inequality has been historically modest by international standards — across both people and space. Since the mid 1990s, several studies have focused on how the post-1984 economic reforms and other socio-economic trends impacted on the distribution of personal and household income in New Zealand. These studies include Easton (1996), Dixon (1999), Podder and Chatterjee (2002), Hyslop and Maré

(2005), Hyslop and Yahanpath (2006), Gould (2008), Papps (2010), OECD (2011), Rashbrooke (2013), Perry (2014) and Ball and Creedy (2016). While such studies differ in methodology, period covered and the level of detail regarding individuals and households, they all conclude that income and earnings inequality increased markedly from the late 1980s until the mid 1990s, with some finding inequality growing further until the start of the new millennium. New Zealand income inequality measured by the Gini coefficient moved sharply from being below average in the OECD to being above average between the mid 1980s and the mid 1990s.[2] Subsequently, the 'rising tide' of economic boom years until the global financial crisis (GFC) of 2008 'lifted all boats', leading to declines in inequality. However, inequality increased further since the GFC and, according to some measures, reached levels not observed previously. By 2010, New Zealand's Gini coefficient was 13th highest in the OECD (Perry, 2014).

Regional differences in income inequality trends have received remarkably little attention until fairly recently. This is partly due to a difficulty of obtaining reliable data at a subnational level, particularly when the source is a survey with a relatively small number of respondents, such as the Household Economic Survey (HES). Inland Revenue Department data yield information on taxable income of everyone, but these data provide few personal characteristics of the taxpayers. Since recently, the Integrated

---

2   The Gini coefficient has been one of the most popular measures of income equality since it was introduced by the Italian statistician and sociologist Corrado Gini in a 1912 paper. It measures the extent to which an observed Lorenz curve (a plot of the cumulative share of income of a group of people against the cumulative share of that group in the population, starting with the group with the lowest income) deviates from the 45-degree line, which indicates perfect income equality. The Gini coefficient equals twice the area between the 45-degree line and the Lorenz curve. A Gini coefficient of zero signals perfect equality and a value of one represents maximum inequality (one person has all the income).

Table 1: **Relative average personal income in New Zealand regions 1981–2013**

Region	1981	Region	1986	Region	1991	Region
STHL	1.16	WLGT	1.14	WLGT	1.21	WLGT
WLGT	1.09	AUCL	1.07	AUCL	1.11	AUCL
WAIK	1.04	NZ	$42,708	NZ	$39,664	NZ
NZ	$49,951	TARA	0.99	TARA	0.96	TARA
BOPL	1.00	STHL	0.97	WAIK	0.96	WAIK
AUCL	1.00	WAIK	0.97	STHL	0.94	STHL
HAWK	0.99	BOPL	0.96	CANT	0.93	CANT
TARA	0.99	HAWK	0.95	NELS	0.92	BOPL
MAWA	0.97	NELS	0.94	BOPL	0.91	NELS
CANT	0.96	NTHL	0.94	MAWA	0.89	HAWK
OTAG	0.96	CANT	0.94	HAWK	0.89	TASM
GISB	0.94	MAWA	0.92	OTAG	0.89	MARL
MARL	0.92	OTAG	0.91	MARL	0.88	MAWA
NTHL	0.91	GISB	0.89	GISB	0.83	OTAG
NELS	0.89	MARL	0.88	TASM	0.83	GISB
WECO	0.86	WECO	0.85	WECO	0.81	NTHL
TASM	0.86	TASM	0.83	NTHL	0.81	WECO

Abbreviations: NTHL — Northland; AUCL — Auckland; WAIK — Waikato; BOPL — Bay of Plenty; GISB — Gisborne; HAWK — Hawke's Bay; TARA — Taranaki; MAWA — Manawatū–Whanganui; WLGT — Wellington; TASM — Tasman; NELS — Nelson; MARL — Marlborough; WECO — West Coast; CANT — Canterbury; OTAG – Otago; STHL — Southland; NZ — New Zealand.

1996	Region	2001	Region	2006	Region	2013
1.16	WLGT	1.18	WLGT	1.15	WLGT	1.15
1.12	AUCL	1.12	AUCL	1.11	AUCL	1.09
$43,054	NZ	$46,429	NZ	$50,178	TARA	1.03
0.98	TARA	0.96	TARA	0.96	CANT	1.00
0.98	WAIK	0.96	WAIK	0.95	NZ	$51,683
0.96	STHL	0.95	CANT	0.94	STHL	0.95
0.93	CANT	0.92	BOPL	0.91	WAIK	0.94
0.92	BOPL	0.90	NELS	0.91	WECO	0.92
0.92	NELS	0.89	STHL	0.90	NELS	0.90
0.87	HAWK	0.87	MARL	0.90	MARL	0.90
0.86	TASM	0.86	HAWK	0.89	BOPL	0.89
0.86	MARL	0.86	OTAG	0.86	OTAG	0.89
0.86	MAWA	0.85	TASM	0.86	TASM	0.87
0.85	OTAG	0.85	MAWA	0.85	HAWK	0.87
0.83	NTHL	0.82	NTHL	0.83	MAWA	0.83
0.82	GISB	0.80	WECO	0.82	GISB	0.81
0.82	WECO	0.79	GISB	0.81	NTHL	0.80

Source: The source of the data is the Census of Population and Dwellings in the years listed. The reported New Zealand income refers to the average income of males in receipt of positive income. Individuals are assigned to the midpoints of the income bands. Average income in the top band has been estimated by the Robust Pareto Midpoint Estimator (RPME) described in von Hippel et al. (2015). All nominal amounts have been deflated by the national Consumer Price Index. The reported national average personal incomes are in September Quarter 2012 dollar.

Data Infrastructure (IDI), which links various sources of public data, is an alternative source of information for analysing the distribution of income, but the population census remains the preferred source of data for subnational income differences. However, the census has the disadvantage that the available information refers to aggregate income from all sources. Smith (2000), Martin (2000), Karagedikli et al. (2000, 2003) and Pool et al. (2005) track income changes between and within regions during the years of economic reforms. The publications by Eaqub (2014) and Johnson (2015) have given regional differences a much more central place in the recent income inequality debate. In a technical sense, the present chapter updates the analysis of 1981–96 regional income changes reported by Karagedikli et al. (2000), extending it to 2013.

It should be noted that most research on income distribution takes a cross-sectional perspective. This does not take account of the possibility that, while the poor are getting poorer and the rich are getting richer, individuals who are in the lowest income deciles may have opportunities to increase their own income over time through investments in education or training, or through labour mobility across occupations, industries or regions. Using the longitudinal Survey of Families, Income and Employment (SoFIE), Carter and Imlach Gunasekara (2012) found that individuals often experience changes in income, both up and down the income scale. There is nonetheless also considerable persistence of low income. Personal income change over the life course cannot be addressed in this chapter.

Table 1 shows average personal income in New Zealand in March year 2013 prices (i.e. the observed incomes have been deflated by the national Consumer Price Indexes [CPIs]). Table 1 also shows relative income in each of the regions for all of the censuses since 1981. Relative income is defined as the average income in each region divided by the corresponding national level. The measure of income used here is before-tax income from all sources (including interest, dividends and social security transfer payments) for males earning positive income. The focus is on positive income to make the analysis informative of changes in the distribution of labour market earnings, because zero income and negative income are typically cases of losses incurred by businesses or farms and do not reflect labour earnings. We also follow Karagedikli et al. (2000) by using male income as a proxy for labour earnings of all full-time workers simply because total income is a function of hours worked and there is much more regional variation in female than male labour force participation and hours worked. For example, labour force participation rates for women in 1986 varied between about 47 per cent (in the Tasman, Nelson, Marlborough and West Coast regions) to about 59 per cent (in Wellington), although they increased sharply subsequently everywhere (for example by as much as 19 percentage points in Southland by 2013). An alternative approach would have been to calculate income for all persons working full-time (to focus more closely on labour market earnings), but then our results would no longer be directly comparable with Karagedikli et al. (2000). Because it is not the absolute dollar values of income but the relative values between and within regions, we are confident that the results reported below reflect those of labour force participants generally, irrespective of gender.

One important issue with census data is that the top income band on the census form is open-ended. For example, the top band in the 1986 Census captured everyone earning $50,001 and above, while for the 2013 Census it was everyone earning $150,001 and above. The proportion of the population in the top income band varies between less than 1 per cent (in 1981) and 4 per cent (in 2006). While they are a small fraction of the population, people in this group of top earners have a major impact on average income overall. This income must therefore be estimated in an appropriate manner. Statistics New Zealand has made available the likely national 'midpoint' income (i.e. the median) in the top band for each census using data from the HES, but this information is not appropriate for any subnational analysis. Instead we make the common assumption that income at the top end of the distribution follows a Pareto distribution. In that case, the number of persons with income greater than or equal to Y is given by AY^{-a} where A and a are constants that can be estimated. If L is the lower bound of the open-ended income band, the implied average income of those with income greater than L can be calculated as $aL/(a-1)$. We use the Robust Pareto Midpoint Estimator (RPME) of von Hippel et al. (2015) to estimate the a coefficients and average income in the top band for each region and census.

The first striking feature of Table 1 is that real average personal income at the national level declined sharply by 15 per cent from $49,951 in 1981 to $42,708 in 1986. This decline continued between 1986 and 1991 (by a further 7 per cent). From 1991, real income recommenced the kind of long-run growth path expected in developed economies. As noted previously, this is based on income data for males, and Karagedikli et al. (2003) show that for females real income growth was positive throughout the 1981–96 period. However, when considering all adults in receipt of positive income, the intercensal changes are qualitatively similar to those reported in Table 1, confirming that the trends reported in Table 1 are indicative of real income change for the average New Zealander. Table 1 shows that it took until 2006 for real income to exceed the level reached before the economic reforms commenced in 1984. Due to the GFC, income growth remained very modest (3 per cent over six years) between 2006 and 2013.

Broadly speaking, the period between 1981 and 2013 can be divided into two phases of regional income change: 1981–91, when real income declined in all regions; and 1991–2013, when real income increased in all regions. The first of these phases captures the drastic structural changes and sweeping reforms in the New Zealand economy since 1984 (see Evans et al., 1996 for a review). It is very clear from Table 1 that these reforms were far more favourable to the urban populations of Auckland and Wellington than to the populations of the other regions. By 1991, average income in Wellington (top ranked) was a fifth above the national average while in the West Coast and Northland it was a fifth below the average.

The period from 1991 to 2006 was a period of strong national personal income growth, and was followed by lower rates of growth during the last intercensal period, 2006–13. In the latter period, Taranaki and West Coast were the top-performing regions in terms of growth, undoubtedly influenced by the boom in extractive industries over this period. Canterbury also achieved a growth rate similar to Taranaki. This could be indicative of the Christchurch rebuild after the earthquakes, which has attracted construction activities to the regions and a large inflow of skilled workers.

Karagedikli et al. (2000) had earlier identified a divide between the metropolitan areas of Auckland and Wellington and the rest of the regions. Examining the growth rate in average income between 1981 and 2013 reinforces this picture of a metropolitan–provincial divide. Taking into account the population count of the regions, it can be calculated that the North Island's share of aggregate income increased from 73 per cent in 1981 to 77 per cent in 2001. This is mostly due to the growing demographic and economic importance of Auckland, which increased its share of aggregate personal income in New Zealand from 25.7 per cent in 1981 to 35.2 per cent in 2013.

Consistently poorly performing regions, in terms of relative personal income, are Northland, Gisborne, Hawke's Bay and Manawatū–Whanganui (see also Figure 1). The case of Southland is also very interesting as the region had the highest real average income in 1981 (16 per cent above the national average) but experienced decline in the following periods, falling to 10 per cent below average by 2006. Although the boom in the dairy sector subsequently led to increased income growth, real average income in Southland was by 2013 still less than in 1981.

Overall, the period from 1981 to 2013 has been one of 'mixed fortune' across New Zealand (see also Johnson, 2015). Half of the 16 regions experienced a decline (from their 1981 levels) in average real income over this period. Eaqub (2014) highlights technology changes, ageing, globalisation and urbanisation as some of the main reasons responsible for the decline in regions like Southland.

Although there is considerable persistence in relative positions at the top end, with Wellington and Auckland having respectively the highest and second-highest real incomes since 1986, there has also been a considerable change in the relative standard of living across regions. A much-asked question in the literature has been when and under which circumstances poorer regions have had an opportunity to catch up to the rich regions. Economic theory predicts that, due to factors such as diminishing returns to additional capital per worker, inter-regional trade and diffusion of technology, poor regions will grow faster and catch up to richer regions. This phenomenon, which is referred to as 'absolute convergence' in the literature, is predicated on the restrictive assumption that regions differ only in their initial 'endowment' of capital and labour. They will then converge to the same level of real income per capita, with this real income growing at a rate determined by technological progress. However, the literature suggests that such absolute convergence is unlikely to occur in practice because regions differ in the composition of employment by skill level and in population growth. Studies such as Durlauf et al. (2005) identified around 145 factors that can determine the growth of a region.

It is nonetheless useful to check formally whether New Zealand regions are growing apart or together in terms of income per capita. Karagedikli et al. (2000) previously found evidence of absolute convergence amongst the regions between 1981 and 1996 once Auckland and Wellington were excluded from the data. Regions with high initial real incomes (such as Southland) experienced the greatest decline in income over the 1981–96 period. Using data from the three additional censuses from 2001, 2006 and

2013, we re-examine income convergence across the whole period from 1981 to 2013 by means of regression analysis. Like Karagedikli et al. (2000) we check whether the regression results depend on whether Auckland and Wellington are included or not. Mathematically, the regression equation is

$$\frac{g_{it,t+d}}{d} = \alpha + \beta ln Y_{it} + \gamma_t + \varepsilon_{it}$$

in which $g_{it,t+d}/d$ is the annualised growth rate in average real income in region i during the intercensal period between years t and $t + d$, with d typically 5 years, except for the 2006–13 period when $d = 7$; $ln Y_{it}$ is a natural logarithm of average real income in region i at time t; Y_t is a national business cycle effect; and represent random fluctuations. The results can be found in Table 2.

Table 2: **Regressions to test absolute income convergence among New Zealand regions**

Model	Panel data		Cross-sectional data	
Dependent variable	Annualised real intercensal growth for all regions	Annualised real intercensal growth for all regions, excl. Auckland and Wellington	Annualised 32-year real growth rate for all regions (1981–2013)	Annualised 32-year real growth for all regions, excl. Auckland and Wellington (1981–2013)
Log of lagged mean income	−0.009	−0.037**	−0.012	−0.021*
	(−1.115)	(−3.284)	(−1.365)	(−2.766)
Constant	0.059	0.363**	0.128	0.222*
	(−0.692)	(−2.97)	(−1.361)	(−2.755)
Number of observations	96	84	16	14
Period effect	Yes	Yes	No	No
t values in parentheses *p<0.10; **p<0.05; ***p<0.01				

Table 3: **Gini coefficients of intra-regional income distribution for males, 1981 to 2013**

			Gini coefficients		
Regions	**1981**	**1986**	**1991**	**1996**	**2001**
Northland	0.4079	0.3642	0.4053	0.4531	0.4568
Auckland	0.3653	0.3621	0.4114	0.4606	0.4678
Waikato	0.3867	0.3566	0.3998	0.4500	0.4497
Bay of Plenty	0.3775	0.3472	0.4006	0.4407	0.4435
Gisborne	0.3911	0.3499	0.4065	0.4473	0.4558
Hawke's Bay	0.3783	0.3397	0.3900	0.4297	0.4361
Taranaki	0.3774	0.3468	0.3985	0.4392	0.4524
Manawatū–Whanganui	0.3834	0.3469	0.3944	0.4302	0.4413
Wellington	0.3463	0.3533	0.4113	0.4570	0.4733
West Coast	0.3483	0.3204	0.3800	0.4171	0.4365
Canterbury	0.3728	0.3492	0.3946	0.4315	0.4389
Otago	0.3857	0.3584	0.4051	0.4429	0.4571
Southland	0.3883	0.3299	0.3805	0.4185	0.4325
Tasman	0.3972	0.3481	0.3810	0.4185	0.4350
Nelson	0.3713	0.3513	0.3909	0.4183	0.4411
Marlborough	0.3719	0.3402	0.3749	0.4078	0.4210
New Zealand	0.3744	0.3561	0.4077	0.4511	0.4615

		Percent Changes				
2006	**2013**	**81–86**	**86–01**	**01–06**	**06–13**	**81–13**
0.4259	0.4409	−11%	25%	−7%	4%	8%
0.4535	0.4718	−1%	29%	−3%	4%	29%
0.4222	0.4321	−8%	26%	−6%	2%	12%
0.4224	0.4332	−8%	28%	−5%	3%	15%
0.4273	0.4355	−11%	30%	−6%	2%	11%
0.4133	0.4248	−10%	28%	−5%	3%	12%
0.4290	0.4319	−8%	30%	−5%	1%	14%
0.4166	0.4215	−10%	27%	−6%	1%	10%
0.4563	0.4650	2%	34%	−4%	2%	34%
0.4045	0.4084	−8%	36%	−7%	1%	17%
0.4229	0.4244	−6%	26%	−4%	0%	14%
0.4342	0.4458	−7%	28%	−5%	3%	16%
0.3940	0.3994	−15%	31%	−9%	1%	3%
0.4055	0.4214	−12%	25%	−7%	4%	6%
0.4181	0.4304	−5%	26%	−5%	3%	16%
0.4027	0.4010	−9%	24%	−4%	0%	8%
0.4415	0.4511	−5%	30%	−4%	2%	20%

The results are very clear. When Auckland and Wellington are included, there is no evidence of convergence in real income among New Zealand regions. This reconfirms the earlier finding by Karagedikli et al. (2000). However, once Auckland and Wellington are excluded, there is evidence of absolute income convergence among the other regions. This is the case when comparing the regions cross-sectionally for the entire period (with the regression coefficient on initial income being –0.021) or as a panel of intercensal periods while allowing for business cycle effects (with the regression coefficient on initial income being –0.037). The long-run annual convergence rate of 0.021 over the 32-year period suggests that the gap in real income between any two New Zealand regions (excluding Auckland and Wellington) has been reduced by 2.1 per cent annually. This is less than the 3.3 per cent rate of convergence Karagedikli et al. (2000) found for the period 1981–96, but very similar to the so-called 2 per cent rule found by Barro and Sala-i-Martin (1992) for regions in the United States. Ganong and Shoag (2015) find that in the United States inter-regional income convergence has been declining. Housing supply regulations have led there to high house prices and rents in growing cities, which has deterred the inward migration that might have contributed to convergence.

It should be noted that the regressions reported in Table 2 do not provide an analysis of why some regions grow faster than others. For such an analysis many additional variables would need to be considered, such as the rate of investment in infrastructure, the average skill level of the regional population, the sectoral structure of the regional economy, etc. When such factors are taken into account, the coefficient on the log of mean initial income informs on so-called conditional rather than absolute convergence, and this coefficient may or may not be statistically significant (see Le Gallo and Fingleton, 2014).

In summary we conclude that, in terms of average personal income, Auckland and Wellington have pulled away from the other regions of New

Zealand. Among the other 14 regions only six (Taranaki, Canterbury, West Coast, Nelson, Marlborough and Tasman) have experienced an increase in average real income over 32 years since 1981. This is an astonishing finding given that the material standard of living improved for most people in most regions in the post-war period leading up to the post-1980 era of economic liberalisation and globalisation. However, the experience of New Zealand is not unique in this respect. For example, it is the lack of improvement in the average standard of living in the poorer regions of the United Kingdom that triggered the widespread dissatisfaction with greater economic integration of that country in the European Union. Ultimately, these regional differences were a major factor responsible for the rather unexpected outcome of the 2016 Brexit referendum. It is reasonable to expect that similar sentiments prevail in peripheral regions of New Zealand, given that greater international economic integration and economic liberalisation have not been effective in raising the income of the average worker in such regions.

However, the focus on average income hides the growing inequality in personal income within each of the regions. Indeed it can be shown that the relative position of an individual in the income distribution is to a far greater extent determined by their age, gender, skill level and labour force status than by their location. We turn therefore in the next section to income inequality within regions. We find nonetheless that there are notable differences between regions in inequality measures. Specifically, Auckland and Wellington have had the fastest growth in income inequality across all such measures.

Income inequality within New Zealand regions

Many measures have been proposed in the literature to quantify the extent to which people in a particular region or country have different incomes. In this section we examine intra-regional income distribution in New

Zealand by means of three common types of measures: the Gini coefficient, percentile ratios and the Palma ratio. Table 3 presents the Gini coefficients for all regions of New Zealand from 1981 to 2013.

Post 1981, we can distinguish four different phases of changing inequality in personal incomes in New Zealand. This applies both to the regions and to the country as a whole. During the first phase (1981–86) inequality declined everywhere, except in Wellington. Subsequently, inequality rose sharply everywhere between 1986 and 2001. Nationally the Gini coefficient rose by about 30 per cent over this period, with Wellington having the second-highest rate of growth in inequality (34 per cent). The highest rate of inequality growth was experienced in West Coast (36 per cent) and the lowest in Marlborough (24 per cent). In the third phase, between 2001 and 2006, the Gini coefficient decreased in all regions and nationally by about 4 per cent. Hyslop and Yahanpath (2006) found a similar decline in individual earnings inequality of around 4 per cent between 1998 and 2004, using data on earnings in the Household Labour Force Survey. They attributed the decline in inequality in that period to a relatively faster-increasing demand for labour at the lower end of the distribution. Government policies like Working for Families (WFF) also contributed to declining inequality (MSD, 2003).

During the fourth phase (2006–13), there is evidence of a resumption of the widening of the income distribution, with most regions experiencing a rise in the Gini coefficient (but with no change in Canterbury and Marlborough), although the change is modest (at most 4 per cent). It appears plausible to suggest that the 2008 GFC and its aftermath contributed to this recent widening, but this would require further investigation. Considering the entire 1981–2013 period, personal income inequality peaked in most regions in 2001. One striking exception is Auckland, where inequality in 2013 as measured by the Gini coefficient was greater than ever (at least since 1981, but probably much longer than that).

Being a single summary measure, a weakness of the Gini coefficient is its inability to differentiate between different kinds of inequalities within the income distribution (Atkinson, 1983; De Maio, 2007). Specifically, the Gini coefficient places less emphasis on incomes at the top and bottom ends of the income spectrum (Cobham and Sumner, 2013). To consider what is happening at these extremes, we present two percentile ratios. The 50:10 ratio takes the ratio of median income (i.e. the 50th percentile) over the bottom decile (i.e. the 10th percentile) while the 90:50 ratio compares the income at the 90th percentile to median income. Tables 4 and 5 present the 90:50 ratio and the 50:10 ratio respectively.

Table 4: **90:50 percentile ratios 1981 to 2013**

Regions	1981	1986	1991	1996	2001	2006	2013
Northland	2.1	2.2	2.5	2.7	2.7	2.4	2.7
Auckland	1.9	2.0	2.3	2.5	2.7	2.6	2.9
Waikato	2.0	2.0	2.3	2.4	2.5	2.4	2.4
Bay of Plenty	2.0	2.0	2.5	2.5	2.6	2.3	2.5
Gisborne	2.0	2.0	2.4	2.5	2.5	2.4	2.4
Hawke's Bay	1.9	1.9	2.2	2.3	2.4	2.2	2.4
Taranaki	2.0	2.0	2.3	2.5	2.6	2.4	2.5
Manawatū–Whanganui	2.0	2.0	2.2	2.3	2.5	2.3	2.4
Wellington	1.9	2.0	2.4	2.6	2.9	2.7	3.0
West Coast	1.8	1.9	2.3	2.4	2.5	2.2	2.3
Canterbury	1.9	2.0	2.3	2.3	2.4	2.3	2.3
Otago	1.9	2.0	2.3	2.4	2.5	2.3	2.5
Southland	1.9	1.8	2.2	2.2	2.4	2.1	2.2
Tasman	2.0	2.1	2.3	2.3	2.5	2.2	2.4
Nelson	1.9	2.0	2.2	2.2	2.5	2.2	2.5
Marlborough	2.0	1.9	2.1	2.1	2.3	2.2	2.3
New Zealand	2.0	2.0	2.3	2.5	2.6	2.5	2.5

Table 4 demonstrates clearly that incomes of those at the top have grown much faster than median income. Nationally, income at the 90th percentile of the distribution was twice the median in 1981 but increased to 2.6 times the median in 2001. As previously noted by Dixon (1999) and Karagedikli et al. (2000) inequality increased the most during the 1986–96 period of financial and product market deregulation. The 90:50 ratio peaked in many regions in 2001. Only Auckland and Wellington have seen further increases in this ratio subsequently. Of all New Zealand cities, those two are the most globally connected with earnings of highly paid professionals in private- and public-sector jobs determined by global market forces. The absolute increase in the 90:50 ratio between 1981 and 2013 was greater in Auckland and Wellington than in any other region. Generally, the changes in the 90:50 ratios are closely correlated with the changes in the Gini coefficients discussed previously.

At the bottom end of the distribution, intercensal changes are similar to those of the other measures of inequality, and peak inequality also occurred in 2001 (see Table 5). Auckland, West Coast and Otago are notable exceptions (where the 50:10 ratio peaked in 2006). Nationally, median income was 3.8 times income at the lowest decile in 1981 and this ratio increased to 4.3 by 2001. However, the greatest increase in the 50:10 ratio occurred between 1991 and 1996. As this ratio is determined not only by the wages of the lesser paid but also by social welfare provisions, the 1991 benefit cuts are likely to have had a major impact over this period. Easton (1996) identifies benefit cuts and the 1991 Employment Contracts Act as important contributors to the rise in poverty in the early 1990s. An interesting difference between the 90:50 ratio changes and the 50:10 ratio changes is that the data suggest that the top of the distribution pulled away the most from the middle between 1986 and 1991, but the middle pulled away from the bottom the most in the next intercensal period. Karagedikli et al. (2003) showed that, parallel to this, women experienced an increase in equality during the second half of the reform decade while men experienced the greatest increase during the first half.

Another difference between the changes at the top end of the distribution (Table 4) and the bottom end of the distribution (Table 5) is that at the top end inequality increased in all regions between 1981 and 2013. In contrast, in the majority of regions inequality at the bottom end was less in 2013 than in 1981. There are likely to be two dominant causes. One is population ageing, leading to increases in the number of people in receipt of New Zealand Superannuation, which is linked to wages paid (the after-tax NZ Super rate for qualifying couples is about two-thirds of the 'average

Table 5: **50:10 percentile ratios 1981 to 2013**

Regions	1981	1986	1991	1996	2001	2006	2013
Northland	3.6	2.6	2.6	3.1	3.5	3.5	3.2
Auckland	4.0	2.9	3.4	4.5	4.8	4.9	4.8
Waikato	3.7	2.8	3.1	4.0	4.1	3.9	3.7
Bay of Plenty	3.7	2.6	2.9	3.6	3.8	3.7	3.4
Gisborne	3.5	2.5	2.8	3.6	3.9	3.8	3.8
Hawke's Bay	3.8	2.7	3.0	3.8	4.0	3.7	3.5
Taranaki	3.6	2.7	3.0	3.7	3.9	3.6	3.6
Manawatū–Whanganui	3.9	2.8	3.1	3.9	4.0	3.8	3.5
Wellington	3.8	3.0	3.6	4.5	4.5	4.4	4.3
West Coast	3.6	2.5	2.7	3.3	3.3	3.6	3.5
Canterbury	3.8	2.8	3.0	3.9	4.0	4.0	3.8
Otago	3.9	2.9	3.1	4.0	4.3	4.6	4.5
Southland	3.4	2.8	2.9	3.6	3.8	3.4	3.4
Tasman	3.6	2.5	2.6	3.4	3.6	3.4	3.3
Nelson	4.1	2.7	3.0	3.8	3.9	3.5	3.4
Marlborough	3.5	2.6	2.7	3.5	3.4	3.2	3.2
New Zealand	3.8	2.8	3.2	4.1	4.3	4.2	3.9

ordinary time wage' after tax). The other factor is that the median wage has been rather stagnant, predominantly a result of globalisation, which is something that New Zealand shares with many other developed countries. Steady increases in the minimum wage may have also contributed to the narrowing of the bottom end of the income distribution in some regions, but Maloney and Pacheco (2012) found only a very minimal effect of the rise in minimum wage between 1999 and 2008 on relative poverty rates. Besides having seen the greatest inequality growth at the top end of the distribution, Auckland and Wellington also stand out as regions in which inequality grew the fastest at the bottom end of the distribution (although Otago saw also a relatively large increase in the 50:10 ratio).

Our final measure of intra-regional income inequality is the Palma ratio, based on the work of Gabriel Palma (2011), which calculates the ratio between the income share of the top 10 per cent of the population and the share of the bottom 40 per cent. The ratio is based on evidence of constant shares for the intermediate 50 per cent in most countries. If the share of income of the middle 50 is fairly constant, then changes in the distribution of income are mainly driven by what is happening at the very top and the bottom. Hence the Palma ratio complements the Gini coefficient by addressing one of the Gini's limitations, which is that it is overly sensitive to the middle of the distribution while ignoring the top and bottom. Additionally, Cobham and Sumner (2013) argue that the Palma ratio is appealing because it is more easily interpretable than changes in Gini. Table 6 presents the Palma ratios for all regions from 1981 to 2013.

The Palma ratio provides further evidence of growing income inequality in New Zealand. In 1981 the top 10 per cent of earners had a combined income that was 1.7 times as much as the combined income of the bottom 40 per cent. Nationally and in all regions the Palma ratio peaked in 2001. At that time, the top 10 per cent earned together 3.1 times the income of the bottom 40 per cent. Once again, the greatest inequality is observed in Auckland and Wellington, where, despite some decline post 2001, the Palma ratio remained above 3 by 2013. In fact the Palma ratio more than doubled in Auckland and Wellington over the 1981–2013 period. The smallest increase over this period can be observed in Southland, which had a Palma ratio of 1.9 in 1981 and 2.0 in 2013.

Table 6: **Palma ratios 1981–2013**

Regions	1981	1986	1991	1996	2001	2006	2013
Northland	2.1	1.6	2.0	2.7	2.9	2.4	2.5
Auckland	1.6	1.6	2.2	3.1	3.4	3.2	3.3
Waikato	1.8	1.5	2.0	2.8	2.8	2.4	2.4
Bay of Plenty	1.7	1.4	1.9	2.6	2.6	2.4	2.4
Gisborne	1.9	1.5	2.0	2.7	2.9	2.4	2.5
Hawke's Bay	1.8	1.4	1.9	2.4	2.6	2.3	2.3
Taranaki	1.7	1.4	1.9	2.6	2.9	2.6	2.5
Manawatū–Whanganui	1.8	1.4	1.9	2.4	2.6	2.3	2.2
Wellington	1.4	1.5	2.2	3.0	3.5	3.3	3.1
West Coast	1.4	1.2	1.7	2.2	2.6	2.0	2.0
Canterbury	1.7	1.5	1.9	2.5	2.6	2.4	2.4
Otago	1.8	1.5	2.0	2.7	2.9	2.6	2.7
Southland	1.9	1.3	1.7	2.3	2.6	2.0	2.0
Tasman	1.9	1.4	1.7	2.3	2.5	2.1	2.2
Nelson	1.6	1.5	1.9	2.2	2.6	2.4	2.4
Marlborough	1.6	1.4	1.7	2.1	2.4	2.1	2.0
New Zealand	1.7	1.5	2.1	2.8	3.1	2.8	2.8

Conclusion

While money may not automatically buy happiness, a certain level of income is clearly essential for avoiding hardship and deprivation. Several recent studies, such as Eaqub (2014) and Johnson (2015), have pointed out that a person's income is determined not only by their age, education, occupation, experience, family situation, etc., but also by where they live; i.e., geography matters. In this chapter we have looked at the extent to which incomes vary not only across New Zealand regions, but also within the same region. Explaining differences in income between individuals is a complex matter and in this chapter we simply used census data on personal income from all sources as a tool to look at income inequality both within and between regions. We basically extended to 2013 an earlier 1981–96 analysis of regional changes in the distribution of personal income that was reported in Karagedikli et al. (2000).

We find that no region in New Zealand escaped the sharp growth in income inequality and the decline in the standard of living that was paid as the price of the transition from a highly regulated economy to an internationally competitive economy between the mid 1980s and mid 1990s. The dramatic changes in real incomes and in inequality within and between regions which occurred in that period dominate the changes over the entire period from 1981 to 2013. Subsequent changes have been considerably less dramatic, though still noteworthy. While living standards have improved since the mid 1990s, in half of the 16 regions considered people are likely to have been individually worse off on average in 2013 than in 1981. Additionally, income inequality continued to grow until 2001. Admittedly, precise conclusions on changes in the standard of living and inequality depend on the selected measures, but clear patterns emerge at least qualitatively from the data reported here.

To some extent, each region has some unique features, and for each of the 16 regions considered in this chapter it is possible to tell a tailor-made story of real income growth and income inequality. Space does not permit such an approach. Instead, it is possible to classify the regions in terms of real income growth and ranking in income inequality. The latter has been calculated as the aggregate ranking of the four measures in intra-regional income inequality in 2013 introduced in the previous section: the Gini coefficient, the 90:50 percentile ratio, the 50:10 percentile ratio and the Palma ratio. Table 7 splits the regions halfway into those with relatively high income inequality and those with relatively low income inequality. In terms of real income growth the split is between those with positive real income growth 1981–2013 (which is the case in half the regions) and negative real income growth (the remaining half).

Table 7: **A classification of New Zealand regions by real income growth and income inequality**

	Relatively high inequality 2013	Relatively low inequality 2013
Negative real income growth 1981–2013	Northland Waikato Bay of Plenty Gisborne Otago	Hawke's Bay Manawatū–Whanganui Southland
Positive real income growth 1981–2013	Auckland Taranaki Wellington	Marlborough Nelson Tasman Canterbury West Coast

On all but one criterion Auckland ranks first. The city had the greatest 1981–2013 real income growth. However, no account could be taken of the greater housing cost in Auckland vis-à-vis the other regions. Auckland is also ranked first on all 2013 inequality measures, except for the 90:50 ratio where it is second behind Wellington (with this kind of inequality undoubtedly boosted there by Wellington's highly qualified workforce in both public and private sectors).

The combination of negative real income growth and relatively high income inequality may be interpreted as the worst set of outcomes for people on lower incomes; whereas positive real income growth combined with relatively low inequality in 2013 is the best of both worlds for them. In this respect, an interesting dichotomy emerges: the worst outcomes are predominantly in North Island regions (Northland, Waikato, Bay of Plenty and Gisborne) except for Otago. The 'good' outcomes can be found in South Island regions (Marlborough, Nelson, Tasman, Canterbury and West Coast). Like Auckland, Taranaki and Wellington are doing relatively well in terms of income growth but also experience relatively high inequality. Hawke's Bay, Manawatū–Whanganui and Southland had relatively low income inequality in 2013 but experienced negative income growth.

Are the regions growing apart, as Eaqub (2014) suggests? Although the answer depends on the focus and also on how we define regions, the findings reported in this chapter reinforce his conclusions and those of Johnson (2015). First of all, Auckland stands out but is of course internationally among a large number of cities where strengthening agglomeration forces have boosted relative economic outcomes.

To a lesser extent Wellington also stands out but mainly due to the impact of being the nation's capital. It can be shown that during the 'reform years' average income in Auckland and Wellington diverged from the average income in other regions, while the regions' measures of intra-regional inequality converged. The opposite took place post 2001: average incomes converged, but differences between regions in inequality measures became larger. The best general statement that can be made therefore is that there has been growing diversity in experiences of the regions along a range of socio-economic indicators. This, however, is not a new phenomenon: it was already noted in a New Zealand Planning Council report of the 1980s (see Bedford et al., 1989).

In conclusion, where you live does have some impact on your position in the national distribution of personal income — and probably more so, the smaller the geographical area considered.

In this respect, the breakdown of the country into 16 regions is quite coarse. Differences between places within regions undoubtedly play an important role in the growing intra-regional income inequality documented in this chapter.

Nonetheless, personal characteristics such as age, education and experience continue to play a far greater role than location in an individual's prospects regarding income and wealth, because the skilled are mobile and move to where their human capital will earn its greatest return.

Sorting behaviour — with the young and highly educated moving to, and partnering in, the large cities — does lead to widening income differentials. In that case those in declining regions are best served by policies that enhance outcomes for the least mobile or that 'nudge' new economic activities to such regions, for example through encouraging migrant settlement or new investment.

References

Atkinson, A. B. (1983). *The Economics of Inequality* (2d ed.). Oxford: Clarendon Press.

Ball, C., & Creedy, J. (2016). Inequality in New Zealand 1983/84 to 2013/14. *New Zealand Economic Papers*, DOI: 10.1080/00779954.2015.1128963

Barro, R. J., & Sala-i-Martin, X. (1992). Convergence. *Journal of Political Economy, 100(2)*, 223–251.

Bedford, R., Farmer, R., Khawaja, M., Lowe, J., Neville, W., Pool, I., & Poot, J. (1989). Diversity and change: Regional populations in New Zealand. Population Monitoring Group Report No. 5. Wellington: New Zealand Planning Council.

Carter, K., & Imlach Gunasekara, F. (2012). *Dynamics of Income and Deprivation in New Zealand, 2002–2009*. Public Health Monograph Series No. 24. Dunedin: University of Otago.

Cobham, A., & Sumner, A. (2013). Putting the Gini back in the bottle? The 'Palma' as a policy-relevant measure of inequality. King's College, London.

De Maio, F. G. (2007). Income Inequality Measures. *Journal of Epidemiology and Community Health, 61(10)*, 849–852.

Dixon, S. (1999). The growth of earnings inequality, 1984–1997: Trends and sources of change. In P. S. Morrison (ed.), *Labour, Employment and Work in New Zealand, Proceedings of the Eight Conference*. Wellington: Victoria University of Wellington.

Durlauf, S. N., Johnson, P. A., & Temple, J. R. (2005). Growth econometrics. In P. Aghion and A. Durlauf (eds), *Handbook of Economic Growth*, Vol. 1A, pp. 555–677. Amsterdam: North-Holland.

Eaqub, S. (2014). *Growing Apart: Regional prosperity in New Zealand*. Wellington: Bridget Williams Books.

Easton, B. (1996). Income distribution. In Silverstone, B., Bollard, A. & Lattimore, R. (eds), *A Study of Economic Reform: The case of New Zealand*. Amsterdam: North-Holland.

Evans, L., Grimes, A., Wilkinson, B., & Teece, D. (1996). Economic Reform in New Zealand 1984–95: The pursuit of efficiency. *Journal of Economic Literature, 34(4)*, 1856–1902.

Ganong, P., & Shoag, D. (2015). Why has regional income convergence in the US declined? Working Paper, January 2015. Harvard University.

Glaeser, E. L. (2011). *Triumph of the City: How our greatest invention makes us richer, smarter, greener, healthier, and happier*. New York: Penguin.

Gould, J. (2008). The Distribution of personal incomes 1951 to 2006: Māori and non-Māori compared. *New Zealand Population Review, 33/34*, 249–260.

Hyslop, D., & Maré, D. (2005). Understanding New Zealand's changing income distribution, 1983–1988: A semi-parametric analysis. *Economica, 72(287)*, 469–495.

Hyslop, D., & Yahanpath, S. (2006). Income growth and earnings variations in New Zealand, 1998–2004. *Australian Economic Review, 39(3)*, 293–311.

Jensen, R.C. (1969). Regional income inequalities and employment shifts in New Zealand. *New Zealand Economic Papers, 3(2)*, 27–50.

Johnson, A. (2015). *Mixed Fortunes: The geography of advantage and disadvantage in New Zealand.* Auckland: Salvation Army Social Policy and Parliamentary Unit.

Karagedikli, Ö, Maré, D., & Poot, J. (2000). Disparities and despair: Changes in regional income distributions in New Zealand 1981–96. *Australasian Journal of Regional Studies, 6(3)*, 323–347.

Karagedikli, Ö., Maré, D. C., & Poot, J. (2003). Description and analysis of changes in New Zealand regional income distributions, 1981–1996. In E. T. Gomez and R. Stephens (eds), *The State, Economic Development and Ethnic Co-Existence in Malaysia and New Zealand*, pp. 221–244. Kuala Lumpur: CEDER, University of Malaya.

Krugman, P. (1998). Space: The final frontier. *Journal of Economic Perspectives*, 12(2):161–174.

Le Gallo, J., & Fingleton, B. (2014). Regional growth and convergence empirics. In M. M. Fischer & P. Nijkamp (eds.), *Handbook of Regional Science,* Vol. 1. Berlin: Springer Verlag.

Maloney, T., & Pacheco, G. (2012). Assessing the possible antipoverty effects of recent rises in age-specific minimum wages in New Zealand. *Review of Income and Wealth, 58(4)*, 648–674, doi:10.1111/j.1475-4991.2012.00513.x

Martin, B. (2000). Sub-national income differentials, 1986–1996. Population Studies Centre Discussion Paper No. 35. Hamilton: University of Waikato, Population Studies Centre.

MSD (2003). Reducing inequalities: Next steps. Wellington: Ministry of Social Development.

OECD (2011). *An Overview of Growing Income Inequalities in OECD countries*. Paris: OECD.

Palma, J. G. (2011). Homogeneous middles vs. heterogeneous tails, and the end of the 'Inverted-U': The share of the rich is what it's all about. *Development and Change, 42(1)*, 87–153.

Papps, K. L. (2010). Earnings inequality and gender in New Zealand, 1998–2008. *New Zealand Economic Papers, 44(3)*, 217–229.

Perry, B. (2014). *Household incomes in New Zealand: Trends in indicators of inequality and hardship 1982 to 2013*. Wellington: Ministry of Social Development.

Podder, N., & Chatterjee, S. (2002). Sharing the national cake in post reform New Zealand: Income inequality trends in terms of income sources. *Journal of Public Economics, 86(1),* 1–27.

Pool, I., Baxendine, S., Cochrane, W., & Lindop, J. (2005). New Zealand regions, 1986–2001: Incomes. Population Studies Centre Discussion Papers DP-58. Hamilton: University of Waikato.

Rashbrooke, M. (2013). *Inequality: A New Zealand crisis.* Wellington: Bridget Williams Books.

Smith, J. (2000). *The Changing Geography of Income Inequality in New Zealand.* Wellington: New Zealand Institute of Economic Research.

Statistics New Zealand (2014). *Decision on 2013 CPI Advisory Committee Recommendations.* Available from www.stats.govt.nz

von Hippel, P. T., Scarpino, S. V., & Holas, I. (2015). Robust estimation of inequality from binned incomes. *Sociological Methodology.* doi:10.1177/0081175015599807

Williamson, J. G. (1965). Regional inequality and the process of national development: A description of the patterns. *Economic Development and Cultural Change, (13),* 3–45.

9. The shrinkage pathway: Managing regional depopulation

Rachael McMillan
Hamilton City Council

The shrinkage pathway: Managing regional depopulation

Population shrinkage is a reality for a number of rural communities and small towns in New Zealand, while others close to cities or in high-amenity locations are thriving and growing. The diversity in regional areas, as explained by Natalie Jackson in Chapter 2, is caused by local-level combinations of birth rates, longevity and migration. Jackson makes it clear that ageing and, consequentially, depopulation is on the cards for many areas of New Zealand, and that the foundation for this demographic future has already been built. We are for the most part simply an audience to forces beyond our control.

Globalisation adds to this complexity by changing the function of economies, driving political transformations and policies and altering the spatial distribution of people and capital. The literature suggests that the forces of globalisation and agglomeration concentrate financial capital, human capital, resources and infrastructure in globally competitive cities while leaving cities, towns or regions on the periphery sucked dry of those same life-giving components. Growth is consequently unbalanced, with some areas experiencing labour surpluses while others experience prolonged shortages, particularly of skilled labour. Long-distance commuting has become common, with people moving across regions to take up work opportunities. Functional labour market areas are changing with this mobility, as people live in one area and work and spend in another.

The consequences of these spatial changes are often marginalisation of more remote areas, in which external forces have a disproportionate impact. Peripheral communities can be shut out of decision-making processes yet still be strongly affected by political decisions. They can struggle to provide high added value to the economy although the area will still be affected by economic cycles at a supra-regional and global level.

Once population shrinkage takes hold it can be self-reinforcing, creating a cycle of multiple causation — slowing economic activity, outmigration of human capital, reduced investment in the local economy, abandonment of properties, degradation of social and physical networks and services, and a reduced quality of life for those left behind.

Demographic decline and its accompanying challenges have encouraged policy-makers across numerous countries to develop combating policies. This chapter explores how governments across seven OECD countries (Australia, Canada, Germany, the Netherlands, Japan, the United Kingdom and the United States) are responding to population decline. It outlines the range of interventions that countries have been using to attempt to change their demographic future, and discusses the limitations of these interventions in view of the underlying drivers. Finally, it outlines key similarities that the more successful interventions have in common.

Although subnational New Zealand has not reached the depopulation extremes of Japan and Europe, population ageing is advancing rapidly and lessons from countries further down the shrinkage pathway can enable local governments and other organisations to prepare for the future effects of depopulation.

The spectrum of responses to depopulation

Central and local governments and planners typically believe that population growth is essential to support economic activity, due in part to having learnt how to manage and respond to the rapid population growth that arose out of the demographic transition. Continuous growth of population and economy became expected and embedded in political and legal processes as a necessary and essential good for the functioning of society.

Although the growth paradigm is being challenged by depopulation and ageing in a number of countries, numerous scholars regard growth-orientated planning as still having supremacy in local government decision-making in many countries. Consequently, depopulation is largely seen as a disaster for economic viability.

This growth paradigm can be seen in many of the government responses to depopulation. In the literature, the overarching responses to depopulation are: taking no policy action, through denying or ignoring that depopulation is an issue in their country or location; implementing policies that attempt to regenerate a location (these may be explicit or implicit); and implementing policies that accept that there is an issue of depopulation, that the underlying drivers are too strong to reverse, and that the new state of population decline must be, in some form, managed (see Figure 1).

In Figure 1, the first two subcategory responses under 'doing nothing' are self-explanatory: denying that a problem exists, and knowing that the problem is there but ignoring it. The final two subcategories are both active

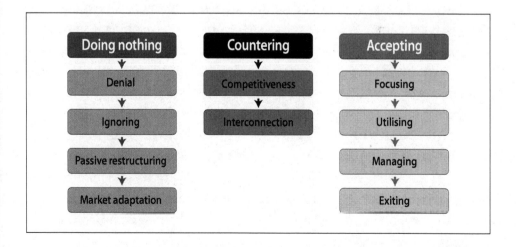

Figure 1: **Spectrum of policy responses**

choices not to intervene in the underlying processes. Passive restructuring considers that market forces will do the job of picking winners or losers, with the assumption that people will leave a shrinking region to optimise their personal economic and social conditions. Adaptation expects that the free-market environment will create a new equilibrium and provide opportunities for alternative lifestyles in areas that can no longer function as a traditional economic unit. The local economy will be able to adapt and provide new avenues for creating value. Civil society will be able to provide support functions where government services can no longer function. Doing nothing is considered to be politically stable.

For central and local governments who choose to take action, a countering response is the most likely choice. Countering attempts to combat depopulation, but from two vastly different perspectives related to different ends of the spectrum of regional economic development theory. A competitive response is based on the premise that competition is essential for growth, and attempts to manipulate market forces to stimulate the economies of regions and attract migrants. This approach argues that growth should be promoted in all regions, as all regions have growth potential, and the focus should be on developing competitive advantages by utilising local assets. Interconnection is based on regional development theory that strong and weak regions should provide mutual support and that to leave regions behind will have impacts on the overall competitiveness of the national economy.

All countering policy measures are aimed at fostering growth. Adopting a countering viewpoint is considered politically conservative. It does not seek to rock the boat overly much, and the public expects and understands this choice. However, the success of such a response is dependent on the strength of the underlying demographic, economic, spatial and political drivers.

Accepting depopulation is less common, but has gained ground over the last decade as a choice in some European and other OECD countries. Accepting responses can be broken down into focusing, utilising, managing and exiting. Focusing accepts decline, with investment targeted specifically at areas with growth potential. Utilising focuses on finding innovative solutions and opportunities in these challenging circumstances — with particular emphasis on developing economic opportunities from supplying the ageing populations with services. Managing tries to slow the rate of decline, retain the current population and manage the consequences of depopulation. Accepting depopulation is considered politically radical. Governments are often subject to short political cycles with minimal policy windows, whereas demographic trends take decades to play out and are often not understood by the government — let alone the general public. Consequently, accepting depopulation can be politically unappealing for governments at all levels and can be seen as failure within the growth paradigm.

The final countering subcategory, exiting, is the most radical. Exiting — or the development of exit strategies by local governments — is primarily a theoretical proposition, as there are few examples of governments actively closing down towns that have reached terminal decline. However, perhaps exiting should be considered for communities that are no longer viable. In Japan, a report released in 1999 stated that 191 villages had disappeared in the previous 10 years. Another Japanese government report in 2006 specified that 7878 communities had more than 50 per cent of their population over the age of 65 years and that 423 of these communities were likely to disappear by 2016. Thousands of villages and towns across Russia, Canada, Australia and the United States either have completely lost their populations or are in danger of doing so. There are many examples of people with no resources to enable them to shift from declining towns and villages being left behind living in substandard buildings with limited services. Arson and suicide are not uncommon in these situations.

Ultimately, which policy response is decided on fundamentally shapes the political and planning framework for action on depopulation in a region. The type of action that is chosen is likely to depend on the issues of the area, the range of actors that are part of the decision-making process (government, business, community) and the type of policy-making process that the area uses. The above policy response categories are useful for policy-makers to analyse their own theoretical stance as a guide to the next step of choosing what interventions to adopt.

Central government policy response to depopulation

It would be expected that those countries that are suffering the worst effects of depopulation and have the greatest maldistribution of pop-ulation would be further ahead in dealing with the consequences of depopulation. However, there seems to be no systematic agenda within the OECD countries studied to either 'counter or accept decline'; rather, a mix of population policies and responsive policies that indirectly act on populations is being adopted at any level deemed appropriate to attempt to change the demographic future. Table 1 outlines central government responses to depopulation indicators across these seven OECD countries, with New Zealand added for comparison.

Germany and Japan are the only two countries depopulating on a national level, with Germany also experiencing a negative annual urban population growth rate (2013). All of the other countries are suffering rural depopulation (2013), with the Netherlands and Japan experiencing the worst rural declines (–2% and –7% annual rural population growth rate, respectively). The World Population Policy Division surveys governments about their views on the spatial distribution of the population in their countries. Australia, Canada, the Netherlands and the United Kingdom expressed minor concern with the spatial distribution of their populations, and Germany and Japan major concern. The United States is the only country of the seven studied that considers the spatial distribution of the country to be satisfactory.

Central government concern does not necessarily translate to focused policy action. Australia, Canada, Germany and Japan have policies to reduce migration from rural to urban places, whereas the Netherlands, the United Kingdom and the United States do not. Countries have a number of strategies to counter population decline, with some favouring active management of the situation and others preferring to let market forces dictate what happens. Some countries have state-directed responses, driven from central government, that force a 'top down' approach in which policy is formed at a national level and the regions are instructed to comply. Other countries have a 'bottom up' approach in which the policy agenda is facilitated by the state, but the regions are responsible for their development plans.

Some countries, such as Germany, have a constitutional commitment to regional balance. Others, like the Netherlands, are emphasising growth-oriented policies to drive competitiveness in their regions.

In countries that still have national population growth, there is often a divide between central government and local government responses to depopulation. Local governments in many of these countries are experimenting with interventions in an attempt to either counter or accept

---

Sources for the table on the following page: Total population, total fertility rate (number of children per woman), annual growth rate: World Population Policies 2013 database; Elderly population and youth population 2013: World Bank (2015) indicator database; Rate of natural increase: World Population Prospects 2012 database. Net migration is the net total of permanent long-term migrations during the period. Data are five-year estimates 2010–14.

* All policy information is sourced from the World Population Policies 2013 survey database.

** The spectrum of policy responses information is derived from analysis of national, regional and local-level case studies, OECD reports and government reports.

Table 1: **Demographic indicators and central government (CG) spatial**

	Australia	Canada	Germany
Type of depopulation	Regional	Regional	National
Demographic indicators — national			
Total fertility rate 2013	1.9	1.7	1.4
Elderly pop. (65+) % of total pop. 2013	14	15	21
Youth pop. (0–14) % of total pop. 2013	19	16	13
Net migration 2010–14 (000s)	750	1100	550
Annual growth rate (%) 2013	1.31	1.00	−0.11
National population decline began	N/A	N/A	2011
CG policy on pop. growth*	No intervention	No intervention	Raise
Demographic indicators — spatial distribution of population 2013			
Urban population (% of total)	89	81	74
Annual urban population growth rate (%)	1.49	1.06	−0.03
Annual rural population growth rate (%)	−0.05	0.36	−0.70
CG view on spatial distribution 2013	Minor change desired	Minor change desired	Major change desired
CG policy on rural–urban migration 2013	Lower	Lower	Lower
Government type			
Governance structure	Federation	Federation	Federation
Layers of government	3	3	4
Spectrum of CG subcategory responses to depopulation**	Competitiveness, Interconnection	Competitiveness, Interconnection	Focusing, Utilising, Managing
Central government regional policy approaches — facilitation type			
Facilitation of regional policy approaches	Regionally driven; some federal facilitation	Federation facilitation	Regionally driven

distribution policies

Japan	Netherlands	NZ	UK	US
National	Regional	Regional	Regional	Regional
1.4	1.8	2.1	1.9	2.0
25	17	14	17	14
13	17	20	18	20
350	50	75	900	5000
−0.08	0.27	1.02	0.57	0.81
2010	N/A	N/A	N/A	N/A
Raise	No intervention	No intervention	Lower	No intervention
93	84	86	80	83
0.57	0.74	1.09	0.76	1.14
−7.61	−2.08	0.70	−0.03	−0.55
Major change desired	Minor change desired	Minor change desired	Minor change desired	Satisfactory
Lower	No intervention	No intervention	No intervention	No intervention
Unitary	Unitary	Unitary	Unitary	Federation
3	3	3	4	4
Competitiveness, Interconnection, Utilising	Competitiveness, Interconnection	Ignoring, Competitiveness	Competitiveness	Passive restructuring, Adaptation, Competitiveness
Mixed, national and local	Regionally driven	Nationally driven	State-driven and state-directed	Regionally or local-level driven

depopulation in their regional communities. For instance, although the Netherlands has no internal migration interventions, in some shrinking regions of the country attempts are being made to reduce housing stock.

For shrinking subnational areas, a lack of acknowledgement at the central government level can restrict local-level action — particularly for those countries that have highly centralised governments. For instance, in the United Kingdom local government is controlled by central government; in Germany a considerable amount of power is devolved to the local level, allowing greater integration of services without triggering central government political willpower to allow changes to be made.

Options and possibilities — interventions

In the context of depopulation, *interventions* are the tools that are used to influence behaviour, whether of people or capital flows, in an attempt to change the demographic future. Interventions can be grouped into policy sectors or policy topics of interest: governance, planning, economic, promotion and social. Some initiatives do not explicitly focus on demographic change, but do so indirectly. Interventions may be activated at a national, regional or local level or may form a comprehensive strategy covering all levels, policy sectors and actors, and may be driven from the top down or the bottom up depending on the country's political stance.

Countering

Countering interventions are the most common strategies; population and economic growth are seen as the ultimate measures of success. Countering interventions may be separated into strategies for attracting and retaining people and those for stimulating economic activity. The dominant regeneration strategies are promotion and place-making policies and economic regeneration strategies. Table 2 outlines a range of strategies that have previously been used to attempt to draw people to particular locations.

Table 2: **Strategies that have been used to try to attract people**

Policy sector	Strategy

Planning	Urban regeneration — redevelopment of existing built environments and amenities:
	    Refurbishment of houses
	    Historical preservation
	    Ecological restoration
	    Public space improvements
	Landscape beautification
	Development of new built environments to attract immigrants:
	    Building more social infrastructure — swimming pools, etc.
	    Developing house lots
	    Building attractions

Economic and social	Targeting skill and job shortages:
	    Education and skills training
	    Industry experience centres
	Youth initiatives:
	    Youth councils
	    Pastoral care
	    Guaranteed job paths
	    Scholarships
	    Youth transport options
	    Internships

Promotion	Migration policies:
	    Quality of migrants, rather than quantity
	    Provincial programmes
	    Overseas recruitment workshops
	    Actively integrating migrants into the community
	Place promotion:
	    Rebranding locations
	    Incentives to move — subsidies, raffles, lump-sum payments
	    Promoting lifestyle attractions

Although economic regeneration strategies are not expressly focused on population, they have been the tool of choice for transforming locations and can be considered to act on populations indirectly (Table 3).

Table 3: **Strategies that have been used to try to attract capital flows**

Policy sector	Strategy

Economic	Building competitive regions:
	    Real-estate-based projects — science parks, industrial parks
	    Competitive clusters
	    Linking research and industry
	    Smart specialisation
	    Innovation

Economic and promotion	Small-town redevelopment:
	    Preservation
	    Revitalisation
	    Economic activation

Economic	Developing the green economy:
	    Alternative energy production
	    Green procurement
	    Green consumerism
	    Industrial ecology
	    Extended producer responsibility
	    Socially responsible investment
	    Integrated waste management
	    Green labelling
	    Eco-technologies
	    Eco-industrial clusters

Promotion	Tourism

On the whole, interventions that focus on new development, infrastructure and tourism have limited success and have had significant unintended consequences in a number of cases. Concentrating on economic stimulation without allowing for declining demographic indicators can lead to a severe oversupply of housing and infrastructure. For many locations, developing the built environment has failed to attract people and has left communities in debt.

Conversely, studies have shown that use of youth initiatives has had success in a number of towns in Australia and Finland, although often the depopulation slows rather than reverses. International migrant strategies have been most successful when coupled with integration/settlement policies in Canada and Finland. Again, these can slow decline but are highly unlikely to stop it in areas with severe structural ageing.

The limits of countering

Although countering interventions are common, most communities focus on regeneration without giving sufficient weight to the underlying population indicators and wider economic drivers. The impact of globalisation on regional economics indicates that the economy doesn't function in the same way as in the past and, therefore, the solutions that have been used to regenerate communities in the past may not be successful under altered economic patterns. This change of economic function has influenced the flow of people and capital in OECD countries and has particularly affected old industrial areas.

Many peripheral areas that are losing population were developed within an 'old economy' model. In this model, population growth was stimulated by creating jobs through large industries — people were drawn to the area for economic reasons. In the new global economy, knowledge has become currency and knowledge workers are an essential component. These workers do not focus only on economic considerations for their choice of location. What is emerging is the rise of an expectation of a certain quality of life, and this appears to be driving rather than following economic development. People now expect to enjoy the place they live in, not just live there to secure employment.

Research conducted in Canada found that regional decline could be anticipated when economic and demographic drivers were considered alongside spatial and geographical locations. The national condition of the country set the stage for the regional loss of population. The size of the country and the spatial distribution of its population were important factors, as well as the country being in a state of low or zero growth nationally. At the regional level, the life-cycle of industries and the changing nature of the economy were significant. Regional areas in decline typically had an economic base that relied on primary processing or resource exploitation industries where the primary input is costlier to transport than the transformed product (e.g. raw logs versus paper, or fresh fish versus canned fish), coupled with exploitation of this resource base at the end of its profitable life.

Settlement location was also of primary importance, with declining towns or villages being located more than one hour's drive from a major urban centre (this threshold varies with context) and not being located on a major transport route. The final regional attribute was climatic and geographical conditions that limited year-round tourism. Over time, locations with the full set of attributes are likely to undergo relative, and eventually absolute, population and employment decline. Not all attributes need to be present for decline to occur.

The literature adds to this research by suggesting that depopulation is inevitable for peripheral areas under conditions of zero or low national population. Outmigration becomes even more significant in peripheral communities in nationally declining countries. In countries that are still growing at the national level, such as New Zealand, rural towns that manage to grow under the new economy are those close to urban centres, with services and with amenities. Unfortunately, this does not paint an encouraging picture for countering depopulation in remote communities.

There are success stories, of course, but these are few among the myriad failures and it can be difficult to assess what is actually being measured as success. In addition, unintended consequences are not always evident until much later on. Although some locations have managed to create positive outcomes for their towns, the issue of competition between several towns or regions that are attempting to attract the same dollars and people is still present. In eastern Germany, previously shrinking cities that are now growing again are doing so at the expense of the region surrounding them, with the newcomers derived only from these areas. Even when places have experienced regeneration, those arriving do not occupy the same niche as the pre-existing society. They have different spending and living patterns and will not necessarily provide the economic opportunities that the community is seeking.

Some countering strategies have been able to slow population decline, but this is dependent on the location and the economic and demographic context of each community. The broad structural trends of low or zero population growth with low fertility and ageing populations, accompanied by changing economic behaviour, cannot be easily altered by interventions. Particularly in peripheral locations, the underlying drivers appear to be too strong for any meaningful reversal. This is sobering, perhaps, in the context of general belief in a growth paradigm, but the best that can be hoped for is to slow the decline.

Accepting
Accepting strategies can be divided into attempts to maintain the current population, attempts to slow population loss, or pragmatic management of the decline. The first stage of an accepting strategy involves trying to maintain and retain the financial and human capital that is already in place in an effort to slow further flight from the location. In cases where the underlying population structure and drivers are too strong, there needs to be a shift to managing the decline of human and financial capital if population decline continues.

Accepting strategies are very often aimed at upgrading the quality of life through renovation or removal of the existing infrastructure. Strategies that aim to maintain and retain the existing population focus on providing a better quality of life, enabling social inclusion and adapting to an ageing population (Table 4).

Table 4: **Strategies that have been used to try to retain and maintain people**

Policy sector	Strategy
Promotion, planning and social	Built environment: Redeveloping city centres for older people
Planning and social	Improving accessibility: Mixed-use/pedestrian-friendly redevelopments Transport initiatives
Economic and social	Employment: Providing silver learning opportunities Promoting high-quality employment for older people Access to jobs, training and education Utilising the increasing mobility of workers to bring money into an area (e.g. fly in, fly out or drive in, drive out)
Promotion and social	Supporting the community: Supporting community organisations Senior clubs Cultural regeneration

Studies show that attachment to place is very important for supporting the economic health of locations. Social place-making has a different trajectory than physically changing the built environment. In 2010, a study of nearly 43,000 individuals in the United States was conducted to determine what attracts people to a location and keeps them there. The top drivers that emerged all supported daily quality of life — the physical attractiveness of the area, opportunities for socialising, and the community feel — in terms of openness to all people. The communities that reported the highest levels of attachment also had the highest rates of growth in gross domestic product (GDP).

Providing social services is also essential for retaining the current population. In Germany, where two-thirds of rural communities are shrinking, it is acknowledged that there is a limit to the services that the government can finance. Both private and government-facilitated projects are exploring solutions where the community can at least partially fill the gap. Some solutions are a volunteer coordination centre, pensioners babysitting children for working parents, volunteers teaching arts and crafts to elderly rest-home residents, local high-school students setting up businesses to provide services to older people, computer classes, volunteer-run art galleries and 'adopt a plant' initiatives to improve the landscape.

Maintaining the financial capital of the public and private sectors is a key consideration for governments, communities and industries in a declining area, as are maintaining housing values and retaining businesses and jobs. These interventions typically lie in the policy sectors of governance, planning and economics (Table 5).

Table 5: **Strategies that have been used to try to maintain and retain investment and infrastructure**

Policy sector	Strategy
Governance	Territorial authority mergers Service and technical infrastructure provision reform: — Aggregating demand — Developing alternative delivery mechanisms — Utilising different types of providers — Creating completely new services — Improving quality and marketing
Planning	Pragmatic downsizing: — Redevelopment of housing stock — demolish poorly efficient buildings, renovate appropriate dwellings to improve efficiency — Improve accessibility to necessary facilities Smart shrinkage: — Right-sizing infrastructure — Green infrastructure — Landscape beautification, brownfield site regeneration — Temporary-use strategies — Land banking, housing market rebalance

Economic and social	Developing the silver economy: — Smart homes for older people — Service robots — Health and medical services and devices — Entertainment — Transport — Financial products — Innovative living concepts — Recreation provision

One of the most prevalent strategies for dealing with governmental financial constraints is the restructuring of governance arrangements, such as merging territorial authorities. Redefining local areas is not only driven by the need to achieve economies of scale but is also due to more mobile populations and changing functional areas. The new boundaries of territories are aligned along factors such as shared economic character-istics, natural resources and common features. There is much debate about the costs and benefits of this option, with consistency of processes, efficiencies and savings sparring with the loss of a local voice on local issues.

Service and technical infrastructure provision is very challenging for central and local governments in areas with sparse or declining populations, due to the large distances that service users and service providers must travel and the lower density of the population, which reduces the economy of scale. Consequentially, service provision is more expensive in low-density and peripheral areas than in urban centres. Broad policy strategies for providing services in peripheral areas are related to aggregating demand, developing alternative delivery mechanisms, utilising different types of providers, creating completely new services, and improving quality and marketing.

A key approach has been to adopt the roll-out of information and communications technology (ICT) improvements and broadband; however, research has shown that although the use of ICT has improved government service delivery it has not achieved the success that was hoped for due to poor user uptake of services. A strong focus on e-government may also be socially polarising, as those in lower socio-economic groups may become further disenchanted.

Another shift that is occurring in service delivery is the changing relationship between government entities, business and civil society. In some countries, civil society is taking the place of government services, especially in severely depopulating areas.

'Smart shrinkage' is a term coined by a number of regions and cities that are focusing on reducing surplus infrastructure and buildings to match smaller population sizes. Research has shown that in some cases population decline has not been stopped by such interventions and they may actually promote further depopulation due to having emphasised the issue to the public.

The limits of accepting

Strategies to change the demographic future are littered with failures with only debt to show for it. In Germany, the government redevelopment programme has been operating for 20 years in the former East Germany. Despite vast subsidies and extensive interventions, the government has found it impossible to stabilise shrinking areas on the periphery of urban agglomerations. Reducing infrastructure to match a smaller population can improve the financial situation of the local council in some cases but can also lead to further outmigration, as has been found in the city of Youngstown in the United States.

None of the accepting strategies identified was able to reverse population decline; rather, many supported and improved quality of life. It is becoming more evident that social factors are able to improve outcomes for communities, as noted by the aforementioned 2010 study in the United

States in which those communities that experienced the highest levels of attachment were also found to have the highest rates of GDP growth. It appears that we need to pay much more attention to social implications and factors in our drive to improve population outcomes.

Success factors

Although successful long-term regeneration is exceptionally challenging, some key similarities are evident in interventions that had some measure of success. Improving the circumstances of a depopulating town requires a series of demographic, political, social and economic ducks to be lined up.

Governance has emerged as a central theme for all interventions, either enabling or inhibiting the ability of strategies to achieve their purpose. Local government policy-makers and planners are very limited in their ability to influence their local populations, as these are overshadowed by national forces; it is thus no surprise that studies have shown the most successful regional interventions to be those that were supported by strong national policies. Appropriate governance arrangements support the other success themes identified: appropriate funding and expertise, community engagement and participation, utilisation of a particular local situation, and strong leadership.

Studies have shown that those towns that decide to take action before they have amassed too many negative demographic indicators are sometimes able to regenerate. The themes discussed interconnect with a range of factors that support community regeneration (Table 6). Declining areas that have the potential to retain population and achieve positive growth are those which have significant factors that can support their community's regeneration plans.

Table 6: **Factors that support community regeneration**

Socio-demographic: — Few negative demographic indicators — Few negative socio-economic factors
Location: — Are on major transport routes — Have high amenity values — Have good services — Are close to vibrant urban hubs
Community — social capital: — Attitudes of optimism, empowerment and interdependence — Viewing challenges as opportunities instead of a 'victim mentality' — A community that has strong leadership, optimism, problem-solving skills, self-reliance and community ownership — Organisational arrangements that foster community participation — Leadership — shared community-wide leadership and skilled individual leaders — Active local actors in internal and external networks — A well-developed self-help capacity to stimulate employment growth
Resources and economy: — The ability to exploit social and cultural capital to stimulate employment growth — The ability to change functions to match the global marketplace — The ability to exploit rural amenities and cultural capital to stimulate employment growth in tourism

The success factors listed in Table 6 describe an almost perfect scenario that is often not achievable in reality. Hence, communities that do not have these factors are likely to suffer continued depopulation that will be very challenging to combat.

The factor that has been the most salient in encouraging positive change in many communities is the strength of the social capital of the community. Strengthening communities and supporting ground-level initiatives appears to be the most successful way of regenerating towns or, at the very least, enabling them to become places where people want to live, representing a high quality of life. Social policies have not typically been used in a countering model; however, research has shown that such policies are a necessary element in a comprehensive strategy. An integrated, comprehensive strategy that uses a range of interventions from both countering and accepting, across the different policy sectors in a cooperative, multi-actor approach that gives credence to the underlying drivers, has the best chance of success.

Conceptualising policy strategies for dealing with depopulation requires an understanding of the complexity of regional change alongside policy mixes that acknowledge the place-based and socio-economic contexts of individual towns within the wider drivers and influences.

Countering strategies can slow or reverse population decline, but only under very specific favourable conditions. Population decline is unbeatable in places where the underlying economic and demographic drivers are too strong. Accepting strategies have more impact on improving quality of life than on reversing shrinkage. In locations that are subject to the full set of conditions for population decline, there are certainly opportunities for local government and communities to adapt to a smaller community and encourage social connectedness.

The most effective response to depopulation for peripheral areas is to adopt a pragmatic, integrated response that uses countering and accepting interventions from a range of policy sectors. The focus should be on positive change while acknowledging that success may be measured in quality of life, a healthy environment and high-quality amenities rather than increases in population and economic outcome.

It needs to be acknowledged that interventions that may be appropriate in the immediate future may not suit the demographic situation in 20 years' time. Interventions such as youth initiatives, migrant integration and business start-up grants may be useful in the short term, but as population decline deepens then pragmatic downsizing, service provision restructuring and strategies for dealing with an ageing population are likely to become necessary. Care needs to be taken, however, to ensure that such measures do not lead to further reactionary outmigration.

There are no guarantees that adopting strategies from successful situations will have the desired result of increasing population when applied to New Zealand communities. What is clear is that towns need to be agile, faced as they are by an increasingly connected world with pull factors only growing stronger, or the market will take the choice out of their hands. It may not be possible to halt depopulation if the drivers are too strong, but there may still be opportunities to slow the progression towards the ending of growth in New Zealand's peripheral locations.

Although each region and community is experiencing its own combination of drivers, for many the type of depopulation they are attempting to tackle is changing form to one that interventions are far less likely to be able to resuscitate. Some communities just do not have the foundational elements to succeed. In these cases, where communities no longer have a function in building national competitiveness, discussions need to take place about the historical reasons as to why the community is in that location and whether the settlement is still meeting the needs of residents, the relevant industry and the country.

At the very least, measures may be taken to adapt to an ageing population structure and increase the quality of life for those that inhabit New Zealand's declining towns. At best, regions can discuss the issues and explore cooperative, multi-actor approaches that deal with place-based issues. In accepting that depopulation is inevitable for peripheral communities, there are still ways to ease the passage of depopulation, improve quality of life and slow outmigration. This does require that the hard questions be discussed so that communities are not left staring down the demographic rabbit hole alone.

Afterword:
Where to now?

Paul Spoonley
Massey University

Afterword: Where to now?

The rise and fall of regions, regional centres and regional economies is hardly a new story. A quick review of New Zealand's colonial history would highlight the growth of new industries and the towns associated with them, only for some to then experience the decline of the local economy and community. Towns from the goldrush era are an obvious example; the loss of Dunedin's power as a manufacturing centre might be another. What sets the current phase apart is that the impacts of globalisation and the Fourth Industrial Revolution are overlaid with the very different demographic dynamics that are now occurring, and which constitute a key theme of this book.

In summary, the structural ageing of the population nationally and the dominance of older age groups in particular regions; the declining fertility that will become sub-replacement over the coming decades; and the increasing role of immigration in providing a major source of population growth, of ethnic diversity and of skills, are all now factors that will determine regional futures. As Natalie Jackson and other contributors to this volume highlight, population stagnation or decline will be a reality for about two-thirds of New Zealand's territorial authorities.

Will these demographic patterns and trends obstruct economic and community revival, and does the new demography of regional New Zealand represent inevitable economic stagnation? This book shows that we need to adopt a new realism in understanding and responding to these dynamics; it also invites new policy and political options. But equally, the title of the book suggests that there *are* options, and that it *is* possible to 'reboot the regions'. Here is a modest list of factors that ought to be considered.

Smart specialisation

In a mirror image of smart growth, there are also ways of envisaging and mobilising options that might be described as 'smart decline'. In growth economies that are increasingly being driven by service and product development/employment, and which rely on innovation, those regional economies that have limited access to science and technology will lag as a result, and so it is essential to have a clear sense of local priorities, and of what constitutes local strengths and actual/potential growth points.

These special target or 'lighthouse' initiatives, as they have been described, are critical to managing the adjustments that are otherwise going to be imposed by changes in the demography or the industry mix. The challenge may lie not only in developing new paradigms that address decline, be it economic or demographic, but also in assessing the political palatability of managing smart decline. It requires a significant mindshift, at both a governmental and a community level.

Understanding and managing population dynamics

To return to an enduring theme of this book, certain demographic trends are inexorable, and they are now relatively well understood locally and nationally. But there does seem to be a reluctance to respond in interesting and positive ways to significant population compositional change. If structural ageing in the local community is inevitable, then why not look to incentivise firms or organisations, or services, to become age friendly? What does a silver economy look like in the regions? And what benefits does that silver economy generate by way of demand and new activities?

Alternatively, what can be done to retain a population in an area, especially if essential services are funded on a broad-based population model? One suggestion, from a review of what influences regional growth, would be that the percentage of a population in the 15–24 age group (the cohort that is, or shortly will be, entering the workforce) is a useful proxy for looking at the flow and availability of human resources and ascertaining whether 'the existing stock of knowledge and skills' is being renewed.

Many regions would benefit by looking at such proxy measures and understanding the drivers and dynamics of particular cohorts (see Natalie Jackson's chapter in this book for examples). The provision of services such as schools, medical care and police will encourage people to stay in an area, and will attract outsiders. Recently the South Otago township of Kaitangata, with the support of the mayor of Clutha, Bryan Cadogan, sought to attract a population (the town had jobs but not enough people) by offering an attractive land/housing package. It attracted considerable interest.

In Canada, regional authorities have developed packages to attract immigrants — over and above government policies that operate at a national level — on the understanding that such arrivals contribute to population growth in important ways (they often include children, who then add to local demand for educational provision) and they contribute to economic vitality. In Halifax, it was estimated that every new immigrant generated the equivalent of 3.6 full-time jobs. There is a considerable international literature that provides interesting and productive ways of considering such options. What is the local 'people and place strategy' of New Zealand's regions?

Here it is worth pausing to consider the matter of Auckland. There has been a lot of regional and Auckland media noise, and dinner-party and water-cooler conversations, about people leaving Auckland for the regions because they are sick of high house prices and traffic. Indeed this is happening, and most readers will have held this discussion or know of someone who has moved, but the data shows that the numbers are only at the margins. I would suggest that regions like Nelson or Taranaki certainly shouldn't be assuming that an influx of fed-up Aucklanders will reverse any of their current demographic trends; one anecdote does not a summer make. However, it's still going to be beneficial if they do turn up, and bring skills and economic activity with them, and so part of preparing for population loss would be about ensuring that the region is attractive enough that people *will* consider moving there.

Human capital development

Studies show that an ability to identify the demand for skills, and then match this to human capital training provision, is critical to the success of regions. The geography and mix of labour markets is fundamental to maintaining and, hopefully, expanding sectors or organisations. One possible approach is that of cluster development (see below for an example), which helps in identifying future labour market requirements, convincing educational and training providers to train or retrain a workforce, and providing a supportive environment for workers. And yet in New Zealand, both nationally and locally, that ability to match demand and supply has been lacking for some time. A factor often cited as a barrier is the lack of cooperation within sectors and between organisations in the same or related industries in regions, so that there is no cohesive vision in managing skilled labour dynamics.

A collective vision

Looking forward, can we arrive at a coherent and compelling regional policy that deals with the new realities of the twenty-first century? Ed Cox and Sarah Longlands recently issued a report for IPPR North, a dedicated think tank for the north of England. Based in Manchester, its research and events programme seeks to produce innovative policy ideas for fair, democratic and sustainable communities. It was titled 'The role of small and medium-sized towns in growing the northern powerhouse'. There's a vision for you.

To paraphrase their review of the lagging economies in the north of England, what are the strategies of small and medium-sized regions (SMRs)? The SMRs must take the lead in identifying and articulating their vision and role, rather than relying on a national government to do that for them. This is accomplished, if at all, in a very uneven way across New Zealand: some regions have a clear and encompassing strategy, and an appropriate agency to deliver on it, while many others lack a strategy and/or a means of delivery, not least because of parochial politics and fragmented local government. (Good governance, by contrast, is about fostering and articulating a united goal, and strong governance is critical to sustaining or attracting businesses.)

We have argued throughout this book that many of these strategies do not adequately engage with the major challenges to regional development, especially those arising from demographic change. Cox and Longlands' examination for IPPR North concluded that it is imperative to maximise the value of regional assets and human potential; another study of the north of England echoes this, adding that regional strategies need to reflect a sense of what will constitute current and future population hubs.

As the chapter by Omoniye Alimi, Dave Maré and Jacques Poot in this volume makes clear, absolute convergence — where poorer-performing regions will catch up with richer regions — is very unlikely. Regions are diverse and growing more so, and socio-economic inequalities within and between regions are compounded by the change in population mix.

As an example of many of the above points, one Danish region (Southern Denmark) has opted to focus on a range of goals that include developing clusters or the functional linkages between firms in particular industries; placing emphasis on an adventure economy; promoting healthy lifestyles; improving human resources; fostering research, innovation and new technologies; and encouraging entrepreneurship. Innovation and start-ups need to be driven by very specific and realistic objectives, and often process innovation has higher impact than product innovation. Such examples as that of Southern Denmark are worth closer attention from those responsible for rebooting New Zealand's regions. We are optimistic — New Zealand has shown that it can adjust to altered economic and social circumstances in interesting ways — but we are realistic about the ability and willingness of local authorities to respond to what are significant challenges for their communities. We challenge them to look at demographic change as an opportunity rather than a threat, to explore the positive options it offers, and to consider how the changing demography of their region contributes to their options.

References

Cornett, Andreas (2009). Aims and strategies in regional innovation and growth policy: A Danish perspective. *Entrepreneurship and Regional Development*, 21(4):399–420.

Cowe, Jessica (2014). Good governance is the key to local economic growth. *The Guardian*, June. Retrieved from https://www.theguardian.com/public-leaders-network/2014/jun/10/good-governance-local-economic-growth.

Cox, Ed, and Sarah Longlands (2016). City systems: The role of small and medium-sized towns and cities in growing the northern powerhouse. Retrieved from http://www.ippr.org/publications/city-systems.

IPPR (2016) Blueprint for a great north plan. Retrieved from http://www.ippr.org/read/blueprint-for-a-great-north-plan#.

McCann, Philip, and Raquel Ortega-Argilés (2015). Smart specialization, regional growth and applications to European Union cohesion policy. *Regional Studies*, 49(8):1291–1302.

Rodríguez-Pose, Andrés, and Riccardo Crescenzi (2010). Research and development, spillovers, innovation systems, and the genesis of regional growth in Europe. *Regional Studies*, 42(1):51–67.

Roy, Eleanor Ainge (2016). Tiny New Zealand town with 'too many jobs' launches drive to recruit outsiders. *The Guardian*, June. Retrieved from https://www.theguardian.com/world/2016/jun/29/tiny-new-zealand-town-with-too-many-jobs-launches-drive-to-recruit-outsiders.

About the contributors

About the contributors

Omoniyi (Niyi) Alimi is a PhD candidate at the University of Waikato. His research examines the role of local socio-economic and demographic factors on income inequality in New Zealand urban areas. Niyi was previously a consultant in the Wellington practice of Ernst & Young. He holds a Masters degree in Economics from the University of Waikato and was the recipient of the 2015 NIDEA PhD Scholarship.

Christine Cheyne is an Associate Professor in Massey University's School of People, Environment and Planning, where she teaches sustainability to Resource and Environmental Planning students and supervises postgraduate research on a range of sustainability topics related to transport, climate change, agriculture, and the contribution of indigenous people and their values to sustainable development. Her research interests include sustainable transport, in particular its links to climate change; decision-making for sustainability; and food security. She is particularly interested in planning for, and the implementation of, sustainability by local government. Christine is active in community organisations that promote sustainable transport. She has been a member of a Conservation Board since 2004 and is actively involved in the protection, restoration and enhancement of New Zealand's indigenous biodiversity.

Carl Davidson is the Head of Strategy at Research First, one of New Zealand's largest independent research companies. He sits on the Canterbury Employers' Chamber of Commerce Board, and is a member of the government's Expert Advisory Group on Information Sharing. He was previously the Chief Commissioner at the New Zealand Families

Commission, and has a career in research that stretches back to 1990. He is the author or editor of eight books about research practice in New Zealand, and he regularly contributes to mainstream debates about evidence and policy.

Lana Hart has been working with employers in the area of workplace diversity since 2000. Her most recent role was heading the Skilled Migrant Business Service at the Canterbury Employers' Chamber of Commerce (CECC), which provides advice and information to businesses employing new migrants, including training on cross-cultural communication, migrant settlement strategies, and workforce support programmes. In this role, she supported businesses with new migrant staff as well as working directly with newcomers to Christchurch who were bringing their international skills, families and interests with them, and was the project manager for CECC's 'Start with a Smile' campaign to facilitate the welcome for new migrants to the province. Previously, Lana was the Women's Advocate and Equal Employment Opportunities (EEO) Manager at the Human Rights Commission, and a Diversity Consultant at the EEO Trust. She has completed an MA in Women's Studies from the University of New South Wales and a postgraduate diploma in Development Studies from Massey University.

Dan Henderson is the coordinator for the Mayors Taskforce for Jobs (MTFJ), the national network of all mayors in New Zealand, working in collaboration to get young people into employment. The taskforce was established in 2000 by then mayors Garry Moore of Christchurch, Derek Fox of Wairoa, Sukhi Turner of Dunedin, Jenny Brash of Porirua, John Chaffey of Hurunui, Jill White of Palmerston North and Tim Shadbolt, the current mayor of Invercargill. Dan supports this network by connecting mayors and their councils with key information and resources to help them navigate their local environment, as well as by maintaining key relationships with central government and non-governmental organisations. Dan was previously a youth worker in Upper Hutt, where he worked for Youthtown. His role predominantly focused on secondary-school-age students and involved assisting the students in their journey through their teenage years.

Natalie Jackson is an Adjunct Professor (Demography) in the School of People, Planning and Environment at Massey University, and director of Natalie Jackson Demographics Ltd. She has a PhD in Demography from the Australian National University, and Bachelor's and Master's degrees in Social Science from the University of Waikato. Her primary expertise relates to the subnational ending of population growth, the underlying demographic drivers of these trends, and their consequences for all levels of government, the labour market, the welfare state, education and health-care policy, and business in general. Natalie leads a Royal New Zealand Society Marsden project, 'The subnational mechanisms of the ending of population growth. Towards a theory of depopulation / Tai timu tangata. Taihoa e?'. Her related research fields are industrial and labour-market demography, the demography of subpopulations such as ethnic groups, and the demography of inequality.

Alice Kranenburg is a recent graduate of the Bachelor of Resource and Environmental Planning programme at Massey University. Her research project explored the issue of planning for population decline, with a case study on the Ruapehu District. Currently, she is working as a planner at the Whakatane District Council, and her other interests include the interaction between climate change, natural hazards and planning.

Tahu Kukutai (Waikato-Maniapoto, Te Aupōuri) is Associate Professor at the National Institute of Demographic and Economic Analysis, University of Waikato. She specialises in Māori and indigenous demographic research and has written extensively on issues of Māori and iwi population change, identity and inequality. Tahu has degrees in Sociology, Demography and History from Stanford University and the University of Waikato.

Dave Maré has been a Senior Fellow at Motu Economic and Public Policy Research, New Zealand's leading non-profit economic and public policy research institute, since 2000. Prior to that, he was a researcher at the New Zealand Department of Labour. Dave gained his PhD in Economics at Harvard University in 1995, specialising in Labour Economics and Urban Economics. His current research interests include the economics of immigration, the economic performance of cities, and patterns of labour market adjustment, for individuals and in aggregate.

Rachael McMillan is a Strategic Analyst at Hamilton City Council. She has worked in a range of sectors: television production, adult education, environmental planning consultancies and local government, as well as spending several years at the National Institute of Demographic and Economic Analysis (NIDEA) in various research positions. Rachael holds undergraduate and postgraduate degrees in Environmental Planning and recently completed a Master's in Demography. She was the recipient of the 2014 NIDEA Research Institute Master's Scholarship and a Waikato University Master's Award 2014, and was also awarded the 2015 Statistics New Zealand Jacoby Prize for best student paper.

Jacques Poot is Professor of Population Economics at the National Institute of Demographic and Economic Analysis (NIDEA), University of Waikato. He was previously employed at Victoria University of Wellington and at the University of Tsukuba in Japan. He is Principal Investigator of the 2014–20 MBIE-funded research on 'Capturing the Diversity Dividend of Aotearoa New Zealand' (CaDDANZ), and previously co-led large-scale projects in New Zealand and Europe on immigrant integration, migration and regional disparities, and on regional population change and socio-economic consequences. He is also 2017–18 President of the Regional Science Association International. He has received various international awards and fellowships, and was the 2013 recipient of the Economics Award from the New Zealand Institute of Economic Research.

John Ryks is the Director of the National Institute of Demographic and Economic Analysis, University of Waikato. He completed a PhD in Human Geography at the University of Waikato in 2002. Between 2002 and 2012, he held senior research positions with the Ministry of Social Development, Te Puni Kōkiri and the then Ministry of Science and Innovation. From 2012 to 2015, he ran his own research consultancy, leading research for the Health Promotion Agency, the Families Commission and Te Puni Kōkiri. John was also project leader for Tāone Tupu Ora, part of the wider Resilient Urban Futures programme of research funded by the Ministry of Business, Innovation and Employment and led by the University of Otago.

Naomi Simmonds is of Raukawa, Ngāti Huri descent. She completed a PhD in the Geography Programme in the Faculty of Arts and Social Sciences at the University of Waikato in 2014. Naomi has since joined the Geography and Environmental Programme of the University of Waikato as a lecturer with a focus on Māori and indigenous geographies and Māori resource management. She has experience in Māori environmental management and sustainability practices. Her research interests are broad and include kaupapa Māori and mana wahine theories and methodologies, place attachment and wellbeing, community-engaged research, hapū and iwi environmental knowledges and practices, and Māori maternities.

Paul Spoonley is a Distinguished Professor at Massey University, and as Pro Vice-Chancellor is head of the university's College of Humanities and Social Sciences. He is a Fellow of the Royal Society of New Zealand. Paul has led numerous externally funded research programmes, including the MBIE-funded Capturing the Diversity Dividend of Aotearoa New Zealand ($5.5 million, 2014–20). He has written or edited 25 books and is a regular commentator in the news media. In 2010, Paul was a Fulbright Senior Scholar at the University of California, Berkeley, and in 2013 a Senior Visiting Fellow at the Max Planck Institute of Religious and Ethnic Diversity in Göttingen. He was awarded the Royal Society of New Zealand Science and Technology medal in 2009 in recognition of his academic scholarship, leadership and public contribution to cultural understanding, and in 2011 his contribution to sociology was acknowledged with the Sociological Association of Aotearoa New Zealand's scholarship for exceptional service to New Zealand sociology.